MORE FRE

Tales of a T

Published by

ROMARIN Ltd
Flat 1
66 Hencroft Street South
SLOUGH
SL1 1RE
United Kingdom

www.romarin.net

ISBN: 0954335058

MORE FRENCH LEAVES

Tales of a Titular Organist

Christopher Campbell-Howes

Line drawings by Andrew Campbell-Howes

ROMARIN

for my mother Joan,
fons et origo,
with much love

Author's note

In so far as this book's predecessor, *French Leaves: Letters from the Languedoc*, had any plot at all, it started with my arrival in France in 1991 and finished with my appointment as *organiste titulaire* – the Titular Organist of the sub-title, whose duties can only be described as feather-light – in Olargues, a village in the Languedoc hills an hour north of the Mediterranean.

More French Leaves picks up where the original *French Leaves* left off. It closes with a wedding, symbolic of several aspects of the large and growing British presence in the south of France. There's no thread, just an assortment of roughly-grouped impressions and anecdotes, not even in chronological order.

Some of these pieces appeared originally in a Scottish regional newspaper. Others have been adapted from a monthly internet column. Warmest thanks to Stephen Young, formerly of *The Northern Scot*, and to Glynis and Michael Shaw, of French Connections, for encouraging reprint.

Christopher Campbell-Howes
Olargues, 2005

THE VILLAGE ROUND

Happy New Year

A is for the *Association des commerçants,* the village shopkeepers' association. Every New Year's Eve they lay on a dinner-dance for anyone prepared to fork out about € 30. It's possibly the smartest social occasion in the village social year. Wow. We made up a foursome and went along. Even at our age dressing up to go out late on a winter's night is still an adventure.

B is for *Blanquette de Limoux,* a sort of fizzy white wine which they serve as an *apéritif.* A false friend if ever there was one. Last year I sadly misjudged things and peaked so early that if the New Year arrived on time, it passed me by. Never again.

C is for *Carte.* Yum yum. Or to put it in French, *nyam nyam. Paté de foie gras. Daube de chevreuil. Trou cévenol. Fromage. Dessert. Café et ses* *mignardises.* Some of these may need a little explaining? *Foie gras* is the entire goose or duck liver. *Paté de foie gras* isn't quite as good, as it's made up of compressed pieces. *Daube de chevreuil* is venison stew. The *trou cévenol,* the hole from the Cévennes – I've no idea why – is a small sorbet with *marc,* a rough brandy, poured over it. It's supposed to promote digestion. H'm. Cheese, dessert – in that order – and finally coffee with something sweet, a piece of chocolate or tiny patisserie. Wines throughout, of course. Magically, as soon as one bottle is finished, another takes its place. You might think that a menu like this would floor everyone long before midnight struck, but in fact there's a cunning French custom that ensures no ill effects . . .

D is for *la Danse.* No sooner have the *paté de foie gras* plates been cleared than the disco chips in with a couple of fast, sharp-edged waltzes, those particularly French ones with whirling accordion riffs, followed by a pair of tangos. 30 minutes of this, then it's eyes down for the main course, and somehow you're ready for it. After the main course . . . but you get the picture. It all helps to shake the food down, I suppose, making room for more.

E is for *Energie.* Can we last the pace?

F is for *Fatigue.* Enough said. Phew. It's good to sit down and chat. However . . .

G is for *Galimatias,* a load of cobblers, which

H is for Hector, an expat Scot and our neighbour, has to put up with from

I is for *une Inconnue,* an unknown woman at the next table, not in her first

J is for *Jeunesse* (youth), who is clearly fascinated by Hector's

K is for *Kilt* (kilt). She says she normally lives on

M is for Mars, but she's chosen to leave her Martian castle for a few days over the Festive Season because she's got some pictures she wants to sell. Also, the Chief Jedi would like to catch up on what the earthlings in the village are getting up to. Would Hector like to see some of her pictures? As chat-up lines Hector has known better, so he replies

N is for *Non*. In any case

O is for *l'Odeur*, the scent of rich venison stew wafting out of the servery. We set to. Normally a little goes a long way, but the dancing has sharpened appetites and we end up eating much more than we would normally. No sooner have we wiped our all-course cutlery on the bread that serves as wiper-up, mopper-up of sauce and filler-up of still empty corners than the disco starts again with a fast

P is for *Paso Doble*. There are strong Spanish threads running through life's tapestry down here. It all adds to the colour and vitality, but

Q is for *Question*. How do you actually dance the paso doble? We've no idea. We get up and shuffle about energetically in a dark corner. Nobody pays any attention. They're too busy looking at a middle-aged woman wearing a little-girl print skirt, the sort of gravity-defying thing you might imagine Lolita enjoying a twirl in. Anything goes for dress down here, even kilts. The swing of Hector's emboldens the Martian lady, boringly predictably, to ask what is worn beneath the kilt.

R is for *Regrettablement*, regrettably, Hector's stock answer, 'nothing is worn beneath the kilt, madam: everything is in perfect working order' doesn't translate into French. There's another answer calculated to stun the over-pert questioner into amazed silence: 'Well, if you really want to know, there's a little wood.'

'A little wood?'

'Yes, a little wood. Just four trees. *Il y a un petit être* (There's a little creature . . . but *hêtre*, pronounced the same, means beech) -

Qui est plein de charme. (Which is full of charm . . . but *charme* also means hemlock) -

Quand il a fait son boulot (When he's done his work . . . but *bouleau*, pronounced the same, means birch) -

Il est un peu plié. (He's a bit limp . . . but *peuplier*, pronounced the same, means poplar.)

Time to move on.

S is for *Sarbacane*, pea-shooter. I barely have the words to describe this phenomenon. Between the cheese and the dessert we are all issued with plastic bags containing a coloured cardboard tube and about 20 papier-maché balls. Fire is general and indiscriminate. There's a never-ending supply of ammunition as stray balls land about you and are reloaded. It's possible to load your *sarbacane* with several: the broadside effect. Truce is only called when your *sarbacane* becomes so soggy that it won't work any more. Hector is particularly proud of a direct hit on the Martian's partner. Maybe he's the Chief Jedi. Darth Vader, even. Quite a scalp, really.

We're quite relieved when the disco strikes up a

T is for *Tango*. Will we ever master it? We've downloaded step-by-step diagrams, but we never progress. Lack of assiduity, of course. So it remains

U is for *Utopie*, an unattainable ideal. The majority of

V is for *les Villageois*, the villagers, who put us to shame with their easy mastery of the tango, although we're proud of our association with

W is for William, another fellow-expat, who puts Fred Astaire in the shade and has made himself very popular in the village not only with his co-respondent dancing shoes but through his complete readiness to join in local activities, scotching any tendency to

X is for *Xénophobie*, fear of foreigners, that lurks in us all in varying degrees. But you wouldn't know such a word existed when midnight strikes and the entire company swirls about the floor exchanging good wishes, handshakes and *la bise*, the kiss on both cheeks, the light of pure bonhomie shining in

Y is for *les Yeux*, the eyes of all present, French, Brit or Martian.

Zzzz is for what we can't put off any longer. It's been a long night. Home and Happy New Year.

Old Chestnuts

We were just watching what they called the enthronement of some new Chevaliers on the steps of the *mairie* – you never know what village life is going to throw up next – when Lazare, a kindly old man from a neighbouring village, came up and asked us if we could tell the difference between a *châtaigne* and a *marron*.

Why, yes, we said: but which is which sometimes catches us out. They're both chestnuts. Ordinary chestnuts – *châtaignes* – grow like weeds on our hillside and indeed all over the valley, so plentifully that they once provided the staple food of the area for both man and beast.

Marrons are generally bigger, with a firmer texture and a more refined flavour. Let's hear it for *marrons*, we say.

Undeterred, Lazare went on to explain the difference. *Châtaignes* have a tiny beard at the point of the husk and a feathery down round the bald pate of the nut; *marrons* don't. Wait, I'll show you, he said, looking about for examples of each, as though they might be lying about as plentifully on the village square as they do in the local woods. But there's never a raw chestnut about when you want one, and the only solution was for him to explore the paper cornet Josephine had just bought at the roast chestnut stall. Lazare helped himself, blowing on his fingers, but the roasting process had charred the husk beyond recognition, leaving no trace of singed beard or feathery down, if there'd been any to start with. He did his best: after a bite out the first, he pronounced it *marron*. And the second. And the third. And the fourth. All *marrons*, it seemed.

We were wondering if he was going to consume the lot – in the interests of correct identification, of course – when everyone's attention was drawn to a burst of mighty singing from the steps of the *mairie*: the Chevaliers new and old – and some are very elderly – having made or renewed their promise of undying fidelity to local tradition as symbolised by the local mountain filled their glasses with the first wine of the year and broke into a Provençal song called *Coupo Santo* ('Hallowed Cup'), greatly magnified over the village loudspeaker system.

The Seneschal of the Order introduced the new Chevaliers to the public one by one, as they received their regalia from the Grand Chancellor. There were half-a-dozen of them: the *sous-préfet*, a retired school inspector, a local historian, a brace of *maires* from other villages.

I'd been conscious of the elder brethren earlier that morning, in the church, out for what they call in Scotland the annual kirking. The village was putting its best foot forward to celebrate the chestnut harvest and the *vin primeur*, the first wine from the September grape harvest. No village *fête* of this kind is complete without a festive Mass in the church, and no festive Mass is complete without a procession of the Chevaliers in their scarlet cloaks, chains of office and wide-brimmed black hats, like so many inmates of the Old Musketeers' Home out on parole. And no festive procession of the Chevaliers down the aisle is complete without a festive march from the organ.

This is where I come in, the Titular Organist. However, French marches aren't quite like anybody else's, because they're a good bit quicker, 140 to the minute. I don't know why: élite formations like the Foot Guards or the US Marines get from A to B perfectly comfortably at 120 to the minute.

Up in the organ loft I might as well sit in the broom cupboard at home for all I can see of what's going on, so Josephine keeps me posted in a series of urgent whispers: 'They're assembling outside the church door . . . they're lining up . . . ready . . . steady . . . WAIT! Something's gone wrong . . . oh no, the flag's come off its pole: oh, how awful for them . . . they must have caught it on the door . . .'

I sit back from the keyboard. This could take some time. Occasionally, to while away long inaudible sermons, we take a flask of coffee up to the organ loft, hoping a perverse draught isn't going to waft the scent down among the faithful below. Could there be time for a fly cup now?

In fact there couldn't, because the Chevaliers manage to repair the flag (it simply hooks back on, it turns out), Josephine gives me the nod and my fingers scurry over a sprightly Napoleonic march called *L'Armée de la Sambre et de la Meuse*. But I can sense that Josephine is becoming agitated. Something's wrong.

'Slow down!' she hisses. 'It's too fast! They can't keep up!' So I put the brakes on to about 90 to the minute – which is the pace the Foreign Legion marches at, incidentally, plodding through all that desert sand – and eventually the Chevaliers make it to the front pews and the service begins. The Mass is undisturbed apart from someone's mobile ringing (Mozart's *Rondo alla turca*, to give the full flavour of the interruption) and a strolling accordionist outside giving the street *Moonlight Tango* in unwitting competition with the *Agnus Dei* inside.

* * *

Back to our chestnuts. Here's a recipe for *confiture de marrons*, chestnut preserve.

Ingredients for 8-10 pots:
2kg (4½lb) peeled chestnuts
12 tablespoons water
Sugar – for quantity, see below
2 split vanilla pods

Method:
Put the peeled chestnuts in a large pan, cover with cold water and bring to the boil. Cook for 40 minutes.

Drain the water and rub the chestnuts through a sieve, or purée them in a food processor. You may have to do this in several batches.

Weigh the purée, put it in a jamming pan, add the same weight of sugar, the 12 tablespoons of water and the vanilla pods. Mix well and heat slowly, stirring continuously. The jam is ready when it comes away from the bottom of the pan as you stir it.

Turn off the heat, remove the vanilla pods and put into sterilised jars. *Bon appetit!*

If you can't find peeled chestnuts, you may have to roast fresh ones. If you can't do it in the embers of the fire, a really hot oven will char the skins off. But remember Lazare: if you want to tell *châtaignes* from *marrons*, it's best to try before roasting.

Cracking the Crib

It all took place in the greatest secrecy, hammerings and sawings behind closed doors, assemblage by night behind thick screens, so that nobody would know what the new village *crèche* – Christmas crib – would look like.

The site had been agreed by the village council weeks before. An endearing peculiarity of Olargues is that, built on a steep hillside as it is, one of the main thoroughfares isn't a street at all but a vaulted stairway, six fore-and-aft flights of 2-metre-wide steps of solid gneiss with massively flagged landings at every turn. It's called L'Escalier de la Commanderie, a splendidly medieval name evoking images of the Knights Templar in conclave or the Three Musketeers swashing their buckles at rapier's length by the light of smoking torches.

The locals have another name for it, *l'escalier noir*, the black staircase. The stone is dark, it's true, and the lighting is pretty feeble, and maybe it's for this reason that a certain element of the village youth likes to meet there, leaving palpable traces of both its ingestative and egestative habits for the older generations to throw wobblies over. At any rate when the *mairie* employees have cleaned up after them the place smells like a vet's surgery after opening hours, all carbolic and sulphur fumes.

At the foot of *l'escalier noir* is a partly-vaulted courtyard, and it's here that the crib is installed. The crib-builder, Pascal, is a small, passionate and stout-hearted man with decided opinions about the way village life ought to go, so he hasn't much time for youths who sling empty beer-cans down the stairs, nor for dog-owners who refuse to discipline their dogs, and you feel that even the village trees incur his displeasure for the feckless way they drop their leaves anyhow instead of into the receptacles he's urged the council to provide.

Anyway, Pascal's *crèche* is ready for unveiling at the Marché de Noël, a Saturday night street market held around Christmas, and we hear it's to be *grandeur nature*, a term you might think meant the *crèche* bore comparison with the Grand Canyon or Mt Everest at sunset, but when we're given a sneak preview we realize it means no more than life-size. A sneak preview? Well, yes, but then we're privileged: an unveiling without music is unthinkable, so my little choir, the 10-strong Les Jeudistes, has been retained to sing the *crèche* in, a great honour. The organisers have asked for two sessions, first house and second house, with a longish interval in between, to accommodate the expected throng.

So at the appointed time on the Saturday night, between the arrival of *le père Noël* on his goblin-hauled sleigh and a display of chocolate sculpture and stilt-walking or some such thing, the village loudspeakers invite the public to the unveiling of the *crèche*. Meanwhile the Jeudistes have gathered, well-wrapped against the cold, at the top of the *escalier noir*, ready to descend through the miasma of municipal disinfectant. About 60 people have gathered round the *crèche*, ooh-ing and aah-ing at the life-size Mary and Joseph, shepherds, wise men, angels, oxen and donkeys, but also at the real straw Pascal has strewn about and for all I know at the real tarpaulins, gutters and downpipes he's ingeniously fixed up to keep his *crèche* dry, because it's due to stay there until well into the new year. We've been assigned a place on the first landing, overlooking the *crèche* and the public: it's been reserved for us by an ingenious row of *grandeur nature* sheep. It's a cold night, and we're just thinking we could do with something like woolly sheep to keep our feet warm, but the shapes hiding our calves from public view are, like the other figures, merely painted cut-outs from slabs of insulation-thick expanded polystyrene.

We give them *Away in a Manger* in flowing four-part harmony and there's something curiously nostalgic about singing this out of doors – well, virtually – on a cold winter's night in a southern French village, at a big remove from its usual comfortable Christmas circumstances of infant school nativity plays, carol concerts, Christingles, watchnight services or other Christmas warm-ups. There's something quite moving, too, about a multi-national group coming together not just to perform, but to sing Christmas in: Les Jeudistes (the name's quite prosaic, in fact: we meet to rehearse on *jeudis*, i.e. Thursdays) are 4 Brits, 3 French, 1 Swiss, 1 German, 1 Dutch – and a partridge in a pear tree, if you like.

However, we haven't included *The 12 Days of Christmas* in a programme reflecting the enormous and rich diversity of carols from all over Europe and beyond. Down here in the Deep South another language runs a shadowy parallel to standard French: this is Occitan, a blanket term to cover the family of ancient languages stretching over southern France from Provençal in the east to Gascon in the west. It's mainly spoken by the elderly and Occitan revivalist groups, and its songs and carols and the tradition they represent cleave to the heart of local people, so we give them *Per veire la jacent* (To see the new-born) and *You me souy lebat* (I got up one snowy morning) and I expect torturing the pronunciation horribly. The Occitan word *you* is what I've known French teachers refer to as *faux amis*, false friends, and you can't get much more treacherous than this: actually it means 'I'.

Here are parallel texts of the first two verses, a little Christmas present for any philologist reader:

You me souy lebat	Je me suis levé	I got up
Per un matinet	Par un matin	One morning
Que l'albo preniot	Où l'aube prenait	When the dawn took on
Soun blanc mantelet:	Son blanc manteau:	Its white coat:
Cantem Nadal!	Chantons Noël!	Sing Nowell!

You m'en souy anat	Je m'en suis allé	I went out
Cercar Guillaumet.	Chercher Guillaume.	To find William.
'Qu'escautos aqui	'Qu'entends-tu là	'What can you hear over there
Gai pastourelet?'	Brave berger?'	Good shepherd?'
Cantem Nadal!	Chantons Noël!	Sing Nowell!

It turns out that what William hears is *lou rossignolet*, the nightingale, which is either a daring stroke of imaginative insight from the poet or a careless mistake, because by midwinter the nightingale has long since migrated to a warmer climate. In any case we never discover what it's singing, because our version stops short at the end of verse three.

At the end a village worthy makes a very short speech of appreciation and invites everyone back for the second house in an hour's time, when it will be even colder. We're not so certain about this: the trouper's golden rule is always to leave the punters wanting more. We decide that if we outnumber the second house public, we'll call it a night; if there are ten or more, we'll sing it all again. In either case we've got time to kill.

Intent on mooching about the Marché de Noël for an hour or so, we stroll down the rue Neuve, passing houses and little shops – M. Gosset's *boulangerie*, the hairdresser's run by Sophie Frimousse (not her real surname: *frimousse* means 'smiley'), M. Bourdel's television and computer repair shop – many with their own delicately lit Christmas cribs in their front windows. Most feature *santons*, the traditional Provençal crib statuettes which many French families inherit, add to, and pass on to their children. There are all the usual Christmas personages and animals, of course, also but the totally unexpected: postmen, millers, nurses, tinkers, tailors, everyone, it seems, except those in any kind of authority, temporal or spiritual, although the occasional *maire* creeps in. No police inspectors, taxmen, *Conseil Général* presidents or bishops here. It's as though each domestic *crèche* was making a political statement, an assertion of popular solidarity: Christmas is for us, *le menu peuple*, the poor and ordinary folk: you rich and powerful people, you've got it all already.

By the time we've reached the medieval gateway at the foot of the rue Neuve we're being led by the nose, by a scent so compelling that there's nothing for it but to follow it unresisting to its source: it's the onion soup stall on the pavement in front of the *mairie*. Now French onion soup has quite rightly acquired a legend all of its own, and I can't think of anything as deliciously welcome out of doors on a frosty night as this steaming, fragrant decoction. Its traditional home used to be Les Halles, the great Parisian wholesale produce market, London's Covent Garden, Billingsgate and Smithfield rolled into one. Onion soup at Les Halles was an indispensable part of the Paris experience if you were a student, or on exchange, or in any circumstances that allowed you to be up and about at 4 o'clock in the morning, but I daresay that since the market moved to custom-built premises at Rungis, well away from the city centre, the magic has worn off.

It's the cheese that makes it so special, grated Gruyère laced with Parmesan sprinkled thickly over toasted rounds of *baguette*, cast adrift in the dark onion broth. As the toast soaks up the liquid, it sinks and its cargo of cheese melts. To eat onion soup properly, you need at least a generous bowl, a table and a spoon to slice portions off the sunken soppets of toast, to wind strands of melted Gruyère round the spoon, and to ladle the whole into your mouth. No such refinements on the *mairie* pavement: we have to make do with plastic cups and no rounds of toasted *baguette*, just onion soup enriched with melted cheese. Never mind, we have the essentials, and heart-cockles warmed, we return to the *crèche* to count heads.

We're just outnumbered by a few diehard groupies, blowing fingers and stamping feet, waiting for the second house. We oblige, but the edge has gone. Second helpings are like that, whether it's onion soup or carol concerts: they never quite come up to the expectations of the first. Hunger makes the best sauce.

Cat's Cradle

Down to the *mairie* for a Sunday morning meeting of the CEPDOL, an acronym so convoluted that all I can tell you about it is that the C stands for *Comité* and the final O and L are the first two letters of Olargues. It's the village amenities committee. Nowhere else in the world would such a body meet on a Sunday morning. I don't know why Josephine and I are members of it. Token foreigners, probably. We take our seats unobtrusively. The average age must be 65 at the very least. If it was a school we'd be in the infants.

There's a packed agenda. The meeting is strictly run by a no-nonsense chairman, but there's a conflict of wills from the start. The floor of the house wants to talk about the mess of bottles, cans, fag-ends and worse which the youth of the village leaves in l'Escalier de la Commanderie, otherwise *l'escalier noir*, the black stair. Fingers are pointed at the miscreants, stances are taken, names are named. Somebody mentions a delinquent whose granny is present. Families close ranks, hackles rise, protestations of innocence are voiced, counter-accusations flash. The chairman manages to douse the embers of ancient feuds before they burst into flames, and calls for ways of dealing with the problem. Solutions in varying degrees of daftness are proposed: CEPDOL members, in passing, should make the delinquents aware of their social responsibilities. *Sensibiliser* is the verb used, to make aware of, usually against one's will. H'm. The *maire*, present in an advisory role, suggests writing to the *collège* to see what can be done. Who is headmaster of the *collège*? Why, the *maire*. So it goes on, and it isn't until someone suggests providing a litter bin that the chairman feels he can move on to his pet aversion, the village cats.

Cats overrun certain areas of the village, manky, mangy, ill-favoured strays relying for survival on the kind hearts and handouts of some of the villagers. Two leading lights of the local cats' protection league, Renée and Simone, are present, listening warily to the chairman as he unfolds his Cunning Plan: if CEPDOL bought cages, say 3, then any member with five minutes on his/her hands could nab a stray, stuff it into a CEPDOL cage and haul it off to the vet's for a quick snip. He'd negotiated a special price for sterilisation – but there was un *inconvénient*: the discount was only for toms. Females were more complicated, so more expensive. So any CEPDOL member would need to inspect their catch to make certain they hadn't inadvertently nabbed a female. To the lay CEPDOL eye, there wasn't all that much visible difference between a neutered tom and a female, particularly if the coat was at all fluffy. Moreover, CEPDOL's writ ran only in the village: members must be careful about catching cats from neighbouring *communes*, presumably filling the vacuum nature abhors and high-tailing it to the village to enjoy an unchallenged run of the local talent.

The meeting erupts with objections. Never mind fleas, never mind tetanus-rife claws, what about any less *sensibilisé*'d villager borrowing a cage, putting his own cat in it, and profiting from a cut-price job? What if a member grabbed a tom that had been done already? I drift off into my own world at this point, imagining an easy catch like Old Deuteronomy in T.S.Eliot's *Old Possum's Book of Practical Cats*, getting on a bit, not quite so nimble, a bit tottery on his pins, asking no more of life than to sleep in the Olargues sun dreaming sweetly of past conquests: then suddenly the grasp by the scruff of the neck, the clang of the cage, the scent of formaldehyde, the needle in the shoulder, etc. etc. For the *fifth* time. I think the village cats will be there for some time.

Some weeks after this meeting Simone's 80th birthday was marked by a surprise party in the *mairie* organised by her fellow members in the village choir, to which all present and past members were invited. Simone is a dedicated joiner-in, so there were probably similar parties organised during her birthday week by the gymnastics club, Le Souvenir Français – something like the British Legion – and CEPDOL, to all of which she gives her time and talent. So she was inveigled on some pretext into the *mairie*, where about 50 now and sometime choristers burst into *Joyeux Anniversaire*, which they sing here to the tune of Happy Birthday To You. Broad smiles and *bises* – the kiss on both cheeks – all round, *blanquette de Limoux* in plastic cups, paper plates with chunks of *baguette*, slices of quiche, salads, pizza, taboulé, all the usual stand-up party foods here.

The cake was wheeled in, a huge affair barely able to support its own weight of gooey fruit, sponge and whipped cream. 80 candles flickered, a miracle of simultaneous lighting. Simone was called forth and invited to blow: *un seul coup de souffle*, a single blow, was all that was needed to extinguish the lot. A formidable lady, Simone. Clearly club membership has equipped her well for this sort of feat. The choir, for controlled breathing; the gymnastics club, for the necessary musculature; Le Souvenir Français, for courage and determination; and CEPDOL, for hot air.

* * *

In the course of a small-talk chat with Sylvestre, a bass, I asked if he had any children. *Oui*, he said proudly, as though he hadn't finished yet, he had four, and all by different women. I didn't ask him what club he belonged to, but I wonder if they issue cages too?

Esteemed Organ

PLACE: The village. One of France's most beautiful. It's official. As you drive into Olargues there are plaques reading *Un des Plus Beaux Villages de France*. There are only 143 others in all France.

OCCASION: The annual convention of the Most Beautiful Villages of France Association. They've chosen to come to Olargues for the weekend. Many of the *maires* of the 143 other villages are expected too. We're promised at least 40. The village is *en fête*. Magic wands have been waved, clearing away fly posters, repainting white lines on the roads, removing graffiti, pooper-scooping after the village dogs, laying fresh gravel in the car park. Volunteers have cleaned out the museum, three days' worth of sweat and toil. The dust itself is a museum piece. The village really does look very fine. Everything's on show, including the church organ – so special that it's listed as an Historic Instrument – and the archaeological dig. A guided tour of the village is laid on for the distinguished visitors. As Titular Organist I've been detailed to man the organ when the tour drops in at the church for a minute or two, no earlier than 5.30.

WEATHER: Perfect. Brilliant warm spring sunshine. Josephine (Titular Organist's Assistant) and I are reluctant to leave the garden. However, at

5.00: we get ready. There's plenty of time, quite enough to scrub hands, get out of gardening clothes and into something smarter, stroll down to the village, collect the church key from the Office du Tourisme.

5.24: There's a mini-crowd, twelve or so, milling about outside the Office de Tourisme. Strange. We expected more, at least fifty. They're wearing suits or posh frocks, not a common village sight. We recognise the village councillors, but there's also the President of the *Conseil Général*, something like a county council chairman in the UK. We know him from his picture on posters all over the *département*. A VIP. But where are all the others?

5.25: We greet Emilie, the ever-smiling receptionist at the Office du Tourisme. *Bise, bise.* (*La bise* is the kiss on each cheek, a French custom few expats, even those who cling desperately to the apron-strings of Britishness, are slow to adopt.) She gives me the church key. It's massive. St Peter would have had a boy to carry it for him.

5.26: We plod up the 65 flagstone steps of the Escalier de la Commanderie. Usually it stinks of cats. Today it's been miraculously sanitized. Magic wands have cleared away the fag-ends and lager cans too.

5.28: Into the church, up yet more steps and through a sort of gate to the organ loft. There's a small space on either side of the console, a bit like the wings of a ship's bridge. I arrange myself at the organ, Josephine passes behind ready to pull stops, we switch on. The organ creaks and puffs into life. Like bagpipes.

5.29: Josephine whispers 'They're here!' Panic. They're here? Already? They can't be: this is the land of *le petit quart d'heure méditerranéen*, the Mediterranean 15 minutes' grace between the announced beginning of any event and its actual start. My music's in its usual disorder. Top of the pile is a gavotte by S.S. Wesley. It's a slight piece, cheerful without being hilarious. I grab at it and get going.

5.30: A photographer appears, nosing over the gate like Chad in the wartime cartoons. I grin maniacally at him, like the naked organist in *Monty Python*. Josephine hides round the corner, the far wing of the bridge. I'm stopless. I bring the gavotte to an early close.

5.31: More footsteps. More panic. No time to find a suitable piece to show off the organ. I start to improvise. What comes out is loud, fast, modern, rhythmic. Somehow it gets more and more complex, requiring hands and both feet. Searching for the right pedals I squirm about on the bench as though devoured by ants. M. Arcas the *maire* appears through the gate, followed by an almost spherical man I've never seen before. The photographer is still there, flashing away. I bring my improvisation to its climax, a dramatic 12-note chord, just as the President of the *Conseil Général* appears, smiling genially and *holding his hand out to be shaken*. I suppose it's instinctive among politicians. They can't help it. A good thing I'm not a brain surgeon. Or a tic-tac man. Or a juggler. Anyway, my improvisation collapses. Another early close. At least it gives an opportunity for introductions all round. The spherical gentleman turns out to be president of *Les Plus Beaux Villages de France*.

5.34: The President thanks me and takes his leave with a courtly *mes hommages, Madame* to Josephine and by

5.35: They've all gone. Phew. We shut down, put the lights out, lock up and trot down to the *mairie*, where we've been invited, as Titular Organist and Titular Organist's Assistant, to the 6.00 reception. Gradually the guests gather, including the village tour leader and his flock. There are accusing looks. He's not pleased. I've let the side down. Where were you, then? he asks. And your recital? We waited a good ten minutes outside the church. If I'd known I'd have taken them to the museum.

I raise my eyebrows. I think of the unimpeachable witnesses I can call. Were there *two* tours, then? The culprits turn out to be the

President of the *Conseil Général* and his entourage. Fish out of water in our deep rurality, they've arrived late and will scurry back to the big city as soon as decently possible. They've missed the official tour. Somebody has cajoled them into at least visiting the church.

We were on duty again the next night, not as Titular Organist plus Assistant, but as my small choir, Les Jeudistes. For their final get-together The Plus Beaux Villages troops were dining at Les Fleurs d'Olargues, a heavenly restaurant run by a Danish family. We were engaged to give a short surprise programme at about 10.00, between the main course and the cheese. So we dressed up (red tops, black skirts/trousers), turned up, warmed up and waited . . . and waited . . . and waited, thankful at least that nobody had suggested that to preserve the element of surprise we should be wheeled in in a sort of Trojan Cake out of which we would all jump at a given signal.

No such diversion. All we could find in our waiting room to pass the time was the family Trivial Pursuit set, in Danish. We'd just about worked out the first question, what is the capital of Liechtenstein? – when we were called in, 40 minutes late. Having sung a selection of raunchy-ish Renaissance part-songs we sat down to our own supper at 10.55. Andrew, 2nd bass and a fine eating man, sat between Monica (1st soprano) and Barbara (2nd alto). Monica doesn't drink alcohol, so her portions found their way to Andrew. Barbara wasn't hungry, and passed her helpings to him. Sometimes things are worth waiting for. And the capital of Liechtenstein is Vaduz, but I'm afraid couldn't say that in Danish.

Bulgar Factions

By 5 o'clock there were four Bulgarians queuing up to use our shower. They'd had a long minibus journey from Grenoble, in the foothills of

27

the Alps, and they were hot and sticky. It was that sort of day, heavy and humid, with thunder threatening. A shower was just the thing before they re-assembled in Olargues church to rehearse with the rest of their choir, who'd also been farmed out round the village to freshen up.

Boris, a giant pony-tailed *basso profundo* in his late twenties, sensibly appointed himself spokesman for our showerers. We complimented him on his French. Thank you, he said: he'd learnt it from his father, who was in the Bulgarian diplomatic corps. The other three had no French but about a dozen words of German between them, enough to say *danke schön* and to hope we were coming to their concert.

Indeed we were. A Bulgarian male voice cathedral choir doesn't come to Olargues every day. We were looking forward to hosting them overnight, too. Boris translated this for the others, and by the time they left, spiffed up and refreshed, it had been agreed that Boris would spend the night in our guest room, at that time a wooden cabin tacked on to the back of the house. It had a medium-sized double bed and an independent entry, so that any overnighting Bulgarian double bass could come and go as he pleased without disturbing anyone else. Beds had been found for the other three elsewhere in the village.

When we arrived for the concert the 15-strong Bulgarian choir, clad in Eastern Orthodox vestments, copes, cassocks and chasubles, purples and yellows and whites and scarlets glittering with gold and silver thread, in-sewn precious stones sparkling in the evening sun – we found the choir loitering outside the church, laughing and joking, puffing away at a last fag before making their entry, adjusting their cassocks coming out of the loo round the corner. We raised an eyebrow: was all this commensurate with their dignity? I suppose if the Pope suddenly produced a bottle of Newcastle Brown from somewhere inside his vestments and took a quick swig before pronouncing the papal benediction, the image would travel round the world in no time and would become one of the ikons of the century. No matter. They were here to sing, not to model ecclesiastical robes. All the same, we congratulated Boris on his stunning, magnificent appearance. He thanked us gravely, bowing from the waist: his cope had belonged to his father, an archimandrite. This didn't quite tally with his earlier information, but who knows? Bulgaria isn't a place we know very much about: maybe it isn't difficult to transfer from the priesthood to the diplomatic corps. We took our seats and presently they processed in, slow, dignified, majestic, with Boris bringing up the rear in his Amazing Technicolor Dreamcope. The singing was equally impressive, Orthodox chants and anthems, full, rich, treacly and sonorous.

All went well until about halfway through their programme, when disaster struck. The thunderstorm which had been threatening all day finally burst in mid-anthem with a terrifying crack and ear-splitting boom, a doomsday, Last Judgement scenario. The lights went out, the stained-glass saints flashed electric blue, the downpour hissed and gurgled, the audience shivered apprehensively.

The Bulgarians, troupers all, sang on unperturbed.

One thing you can count on in Catholic churches is a ready supply of candles. M. Arcas the *maire* took silent charge, one of the choir produced a box of matches from somewhere inside his vestments, and presently a tiny candle flame appeared up by the altar. Soon others appeared here and there, lit from the first, and then more and more, in a sort of arithmetical progression, until the church was suffused with a warm, gentle light, comfortable and reassuring against the raging storm outside. And still the Bulgarians sang on.

The whole village had been deprived of electricity, so the post-concert *verre d'amitié* – the glass of friendship – for performers and public alike in the *mairie* was also candle-lit. These usually very civilised receptions are free, unless you count listening to the inevitable speeches as a hidden charge, but the subsequent turn of events was as cataclysmic as the thunderstorm and twice as bizarre: the Bulgarian conductor, a squat, fiery man, replied in French to M. Arcas' gracious speech of thanks and congratulation with a savage denunciation of the Allied – and particularly the French – peacekeeping role in Kosovo. The Allies supported the wrong side, he said. They should have bombed the Albanians out of existence. The Allies would pay dearly for it. The French would get the comeuppance they so signally deserved, no doubt about it. The conflict wasn't over yet, not by a long chalk, mark his words.

Silence. Consternation. A German lady stood up to denounce the shameful impropriety of such remarks in any circumstances, let alone after a concert of sacred music, not to mention while eating and drinking at the village's expense. There was some sporadic applause from people not really wanting to get involved in this sort of argument. The Bulgarian choir stood mute and unmoved, their lack of reaction doubly explained by not understanding French and by knowing which side their bread was buttered on.

But Boris had other things than genocide on his mind. Still coped, cassocked and chasubled, he came up to me during the embarrassed shuffling and murmuring and asked conspiratorially if he could have a quiet word. Would we mind if the hosting arrangements were changed slightly? Could he possibly double up in our guest room with another person?

It's up to you, we said, but it's not a very big bed. It'll be pretty cramped.

Oh, don't worry: I expect we'll get by, he replied. I'll introduce you.

Hoping he wasn't proposing to bring the genocidal conductor under our roof, we followed him in the dim light through the crowd of vestmented Bulgars and erstwhile audience. Sitting on a window seat, lit by lightning flashes, was a trim, pretty blonde of about 20 in a white dress.

Aha.

Boris introduced her as Arlette, a French music student with a strong penchant for Eastern Orthodox music. And for its practitioners, clearly. We shook hands and left them with instructions to come on when they were ready. They appeared just after midnight, Boris with a bottle of rift-healing Bulgarian wine from his father's estates. Arlette, who was having no end of a week following the choir on its French tour, mentioned that she believed his father was a surgeon, and we agreed that he was clearly a man of parts. We fell to talking, and whether it was the wine, the bubbly presence of Arlette, the fact that we had a common language rather than plowtering about in scrips and scraps of German or Russian, or whether Boris felt he ought to do penance for the bomb-happy conductor, it was 2am before he and Arlette disappeared arm in arm to their narrow bed. By that time we'd learnt that the conductor lived no nearer Bulgaria than we did, a mere third of the choir actually sang in churches in Bulgaria, that the rest were makeweights or had come along for the ride. Boris himself was an opera singer, taking a week between roles to help out. None of the choir was entitled to wear priestly robes, they just wore borrowed vestments for the effect.

We too retired, our overview of Bulgaria not much edified by the evening's experiences. If they operated at this level of illusion, they probably brought the storm with them as a theatrical prop. I wouldn't put it past them.

Polling day

The tricolor is flying outside the *mairie*, the village town hall, flopping idly in the soft spring breeze. Sunning himself at the top of the steps is Jean-Claude, looking like a prosperous antiquarian taking a breather in the shop doorway and scanning the pavements for custom, and we're pleased to see him, because we know him well: he sings bass in my choir.

Indeed, maybe the Mairie will be his shop doorway, in a manner of speaking, later that evening when the poll has closed and the vote-counting has finished, because Jean-Claude is up for election as a municipal councillor. It's a big day for him, he's taken his destiny in both hands: talented and hard-working organiser though he is, he's relatively new to the village, and he's from the north, from *la région parisienne*, both handicaps in the Midi when it comes to getting the locals to vote for you. However, maybe he's holding a trump card: the *maire*, who's fairly certain of getting back in, has asked Jean-Claude to stand, and the *maire's* endorsement is probably as good as a couple of hundred votes in a village where there are only about 450 voters.

We shake hands with Jean-Claude, go in, and we're surprised to be greeted with a cheer from the officials on duty, not something we ever remember from voting experiences in the UK. But then the village election team isn't much like the dour and unsmiling polling station officials we've been used to: it's more like an end-of-term bash with the outgoing *maire*, hand on the shutter of the ballot box, presiding over his own possible re-election, several outgoing councillors and village elders dealing with the paperwork and the *maire's* one opponent seeing fair play. They seem to be having a high old time of it. Admittedly, it's 3 o'clock on a Sunday afternoon, not long after lunch.

But the cheer we get is because it's our First Time. We haven't been able to vote in French elections until now. We're about to lose our democratic virginity, a pretty exciting prospect at our advanced age. We're the only Brits in the village on the electoral register. In fact our numbers on the roll of foreign residents entitled to vote in local elections are 1 and 2. Josette Fornairon, the outgoing *maire adjoint* or deputy on duty with the electoral registers, asks us for our numbers. We tell her, feeling – in this respect – like Lenin or Trotsky quoting their communist party membership numbers. She refuses to believe us. *C'est pas possible*, she says, it's not possible: how can two foreign Johnny-come-latelies be Numbers 1 and 2 on the electoral roll? Geneviève Fau, ever-efficient secretary at the *mairie*, draws her attention to a second, ultra-slim register of foreign residents entitled to vote, and there we are.

Jean-Claude, always the willing guide, gives us two printed lists, the first with 15 names on it, including his own, headed by the outgoing *maire*, and if they're elected *en bloc* they'll form the new council. But there's a second, rival list, with only four names on it. These are our ballot papers. We can choose a maximum of 15 people from the 19 candidates on offer. There seem to be 6 options.

Option 1: We can make our choice by crossing off the unwanted candidates and leaving unmarked those we do want.

Option 2: We can simply throw away the list we don't want and retain the one we do.

Option 3: We can mix and match from both lists, just as long as our choice doesn't exceed 15.

Option 4: If we're thoroughly cheesed off with the whole lot of them, we can cross everybody's name out.

Clear so far? Very good. On we go.

Option 5: If we want to vote for somebody completely different, Jean-Claude tells us, we're free to write in his/her name by hand, just as long as our candidate is on the village electoral roll and isn't currently in prison.

Option 6: If we find all this is too bizarre or complicated, especially in view of the splendid Sunday lunch we've just enjoyed along the road at Le Châtaignon, we can just shove off home and not bother. This option seems a bit defeatist, however, so we hand over our election cards, determined to go all the way, and the *maire* gives us each an orange envelope printed REPUBLIQUE FRANÇAISE.

We go into the polling booth. There aren't any pencils, but there is a waste-paper basket. It's overflowing: most people seem to have taken up Option 2 and have binned one or other of the lists. Even without furtively riffling through the rejects it's easy to see the voting trend. Jean-Claude needn't worry too much.

I do the necessary (I can't speak for Josephine), and put my paper into the orange envelope. We emerge from the booths simultaneously, the *maire* opens the slot in the ballot box, we drop our envelopes in as he pronounces the formula *a voté* (has voted), sign the register, reclaim our voting cards for the next go in six years' time, shake hands with the end-of-termers and go home, reeling. Phew. Did we reel home in much the same way after other losses of innocence?

* * *

We went to look at the results pinned on the Mairie door a couple of days later. As expected, all the retiring *maire's* list got in. None of the rival four did. Jean-Claude made it comfortably by some 40 votes. But what struck us most was the Option 5 factor, extra names that people had added by hand to their ballot papers. There were FIFTY of them, all with one or two votes. Had there been a brisk trade in people voting for themselves? Why, Josephine and I could have voted for each other as well as for ourselves, if only we'd thought of it. That way we'd have had two votes each, equalling the tally of Françoise, our dentist's wife, who wasn't even there to vote. Nor was her husband Pierre, who only got one vote. Had he been a bit too handy with the drill with one of his patients?

Alexa, receptionist at the local environmental centre, also got one vote, and I think she was pretty pleased, although her analysis was swift and pithy: *C'est un admirateur secret,* she said. *Ou un crétin.*

EVENTS

Fair enough

SCENE: Montpellier, super-sophisticate among Mediterranean cities. Only Venice and Barcelona offer any challenge.

OCCASION: La Comédie du Livre, the annual 3-day Book Fair. It's called 'Comédie' because it takes place out of doors, pavilioned in splendour at one end of the immense, traffic-free Place de la Comédie, itself named after the gorgeous Second Empire opera house, the Opéra-Comédie, dominating the other end. The Fair was supposed to have a Chinese flavour this year, but the outbreak of SARS kept Chinese guests at home. All the same, there are about eighty exhibitors.

WEATHER: Desperate. *Tramontane* – we're too far west for the more famous *mistral* – coming down from the heights of the Cévennes like the wolf on the fold. Steady rain forming rivulets between stacks of books.

CAST: Winston, proprietor of The Bookshop, an English bookstore in Montpellier. There's a surprising demand for books in English. Elizabeth, an American faith novelist, signing her books. Yours truly, ditto. Helga, a stunning Icelandic girl. Mousse, a drunken

Frenchman, not a common sight in the Midi. A misinformed Spanish woman. A lecherous Moroccan. You can't say we're not cosmopolitan down here.

Episode 1: Mousse staggers up to our tented stall. What teeth he's got are like Stonehenge. He has something unappealing, a crab or an eel, writhing in a plastic bag. He loves England, he says. More than anybody else he loves Major . . . Major . . . he searches vainly for the name. Thompson? I suggest, thinking of the pin-striped, bowler-hatted and umbrella'd stereotype Englishman invented by Pierre Daninos. Mousse is disappointed to learn that Daninos was French. Mousse holds the whole French nation in contempt. He makes a rude one-fingered gesture to express his feelings for France. I tell him the same gesture in the UK requires two fingers. He staggers off, laughing uncontrollably. This is compelling evidence that England is doubly superior to France.

Episode 2: Helga appears. She is very, very beautiful. She has just been to the SARS-free Chinese calligrapher in a nearby pavilion. She shows us some sheets of paper with Chinese characters brushed on them. They are her name, she says. How can you tell? Winston asks: for all you know they might say 'Ugly woman here' or even 'Dog turds'. Winston has a way with beautiful Icelandic women, he can get away with this sort of thing. I'm reminded of an ample-bosomed Englishwoman visiting Hong Kong who despite strong discouragement insisted on having some material she found printed with Chinese characters made up into a blouse. Later she discovered the characters said 'full-cream milk'. H'm. Helga buys a copy of Jane Austen's *Emma*, unpredictably a best-seller at the Book Fair. Maybe it's a Montpellier university set text.

Episode 3: Mousse re-appears. His bag is empty. He's thought of another famous English writer. Sha . . .Sha . . . he gives up. Shakespeare? I suggest. That's the one, he says: To be or not to be. My god, he loves that man. He shambles off, but it won't be the last we see of him. What draws drunks to our tent?

Episode 4: An bustling Spanish woman arrives, flourishing a sheet of paper. She wants our autographs. She says she's going round the tents collecting the signatures of 'all you famous intellectuals'. She wants them for her son. They might be worth a lot of money one day. Winston and I look at each other, eyebrows raised. Now's our chance. How shall we sign ourselves? Which famous intellectuals might we have been, but for the accident of our birth? Noam Chomsky? Raymond Queneau? Gramsci? Derrida? We come to the conclusion that you can't be a famous intellectual until you're dead, so we chicken out and sign our own names, consigning her son to certain but decent poverty. It was nice to be asked, though.

Episode 5: A pair of municipal policemen approach Winston and tell him they've caught somebody red-handed, stealing from a display stand of small books. They've got him the other side of the avenue. Will Winston please come over, identify his property and press charges? Winston follows them over to a knot of excited security guards, cock-a-hoop with their prey. There's a cringing young Moroccan, wrists manacled behind his back, clearly a desperate criminal. He's stolen a book priced at 6 euros, about £4. Winston, kindly soul, is uncertain about pressing charges, but the municipal police say he can't be allowed to get away with it. Winston eventually agrees. The culprit offers to pay for the book, an empty gesture because it turns out he hasn't got any money. He's told to return the book, he's put under an immediate *interdiction* from the city centre and is carted off to the nick to be charged.

Full of admiration for the vigilance of the security guards, Winston returns to the tent with the recovered book. Naturally it's in English, not a language the culprit is familiar with. There are a couple of pictures, neither very suggestive. He holds it up to show us: it's a very abridged version of the *Kama Sutra*.

Episode 6: Elizabeth appears. She's a pretty, petite, soignée American who lives locally. She takes up station behind a stack of her novels, including her latest, *The Swan House*. Some are in translation:

37

Dutch, German, Norwegian, but none it seems in Spanish or Icelandic. Mousse, moth to the flame, re-appears. Shamefully, I hide behind a display of pulp fiction, pretending to be busy. He won't go. The more charm and tact Elizabeth shows him, the more he's fascinated and the longer he stays. He's putting off other customers too, even French children – and adults – fascinated by piles of Harry Potter books in the original English. He'll have to go. But how? We can hardly frog-march him, wriggling like the thing he had in his bag, to the other end of the Place de la Comédie and dump him in the fountain until he sobers up.

Winston, ever resourceful, comes to the rescue. Although he's standing not two metres away from Elizabeth, he rings her on his mobile. She excuses herself from Mousse, carries on a long, meaningless telephone conversation with Winston, during which Mousse drifts off and we never see him again. I wish I'd thought of that. Maybe I would if I'd been a famous intellectual.

Revolting habits

There's a first time for everything. Catching measles, eating oysters or spinach, riding a bike without stabilisers, baking an uncollapsed sponge, your first unassisted length of the pool, uttering a virgin *merci* or *bonjour* on your first visit to France, not to mention some of life's richer passionate eyes-closed dynamite experiences. Add to the list, if you want.

We notched up a first the other day, even at our advanced age. Not too much eyes-closed passion about it, I'm afraid: we went on a protest march, something we'd never done before. The nearest we'd ever come to registering public disapproval, apart from putting the world to rights in the pub, was signing the occasional petition.

There's a big stushie going on along our valley about a proposal to create a giant rubbish dump in a disused quarry up in the hills between St Pons and St Chinian. It's supposed to be for dead-end rubbish that can't be economically recycled, what they call *ultimes déchets*. In the villages along the valley we're asked to sort out our rubbish, separating out the glass, paper, metal and plastic containers into special hoppers ready for recycling. Sale of recyclable material is supposed to keep down costs, but there isn't much evidence of it in the annual bill for rubbish clearance. Everything else – banana skins, oyster shells, coffee grounds, dust, corks, old shoes, you name it – becomes *ultimes déchets* and is bagged up and dumped in wheelie-bins about the village. A quick glance inside any of the village wheelie-bins reveals the French genius for non-conformity.

Ultimes déchets used to be carted off to the local dump, high above the village, and there aren't any prizes for guessing why even the *maire* called this unlovely, stench-ridden, smoke-girt fastness Mont Vésuve.

But Mont Vésuve's days were numbered. There was a closure order on it, along with all the other mini-dumps in the area, and quite right too. Hence the need to find a new maxi-dump. But where? This is an area of outstanding natural beauty, so much so that they've designated it Le Parc Natural Régional du Haut Languedoc, the High Languedoc – oh, come on, you can translate it yourself. Parks and dumps don't mix. We're daily expecting a new franglais term to appear, *le nimbyisme*. Maybe it already has. So there's good carrion here for the protesters. Some groups are impressively well organised, others create as much pollution with roadside daubings and fly posting as they fear will ooze out from the new dump.

Anyway, we went along to St Pons one Saturday afternoon to march in support of the anti-dumpers, an event the French call *une manifestation, manif* for short. There was a carnival atmosphere, the sun shone, stalls sold home produce in aid of protest funds, little children dressed as *ultimes déchets* ran about, bands played, eyes-closed passionate speeches in French and Occitan, the ancient language of the Midi, poured from a gaily decorated podium. The march set off, about 2000 strong, banners and placards held aloft, singing, laughing, shouting cheery greetings to friends at upper windows or a few ranks behind. We were somewhere in the middle, sandwiched between the brass band at the head and an accordion duo playing folk dance tunes behind us. Good fun.

The *préfet*, the President's man in the *département*, had banned the march from the Grand' Rue, so we obediently kept to the back streets. The only hint of the traditional French gift for protest and public disorder appeared in crossing the Grand' Rue, when ranks seven or eight broad narrowed to a funeral-paced single file, in order to hold the traffic up for as long as possible. If you have anything of a subversive streak in you, this can be quite good fun. If you're a driver in a hurry, it's perfectly infuriating.

The march reformed by the hospital and set off back to the cathedral square, led by the children and some floats decorated to show the effects of ill-placed rubbish dumps. A concert followed, with bands and singing, and presently everyone went home, having had a very nice time.

Too nice, really. If you want to make a political point, even for something as local as the siting of the area tip, you have to use all the clout at your disposal. There's an example close at hand: José Bové, president of a body called La Confédération Paysanne, a guild of small farmers, lives not far away, a much respected rural militant on his way to becoming a cult figure. At least, he lives not far away when he isn't doing time for demolishing American-style burger eateries or publicly slashing stands of genetically modified maize.

A sturdy, moustached man reminiscent – apart from his trademark pipe – of Vercingetorix or other Gallic folk-hero, José Bové is clearly a professional of the first water. When summoned to report to Montpellier's equivalent of Wormwood Scrubs or Sing Sing to start a stretch, he drove down from his farm in the hills on his tractor, followed by sympathisers. Result? Traffic chaos, all the way to the slammer.

The dump protest is probably too local for José Bové to take any active leadership. In any case the charge has been sounded by a gentle beekeeper, who has realised, maybe after consultation with his bees, that rubbish disposal is much more complicated than simply finding a big enough hole to put it all in, and that the real battlefield lies not along St Pons High Street but in the law courts. The law's delays are no less proverbial here than anywhere else, and while the case drags on the entrance to the proposed dump remains closed and all our *ultimes déchets* are carted off to the Yonne *département*, 700 kilometres away. A triumph of *nimbyisme*.

Meanwhile the valley authorities have taken over a small vineyard and have built a *déchetterie*, a drive-in garbageorama with hoppers for cardboard, builder's rubble, old iron, noxious chemicals, sumpoil, garden refuse, everything except *ultimes déchets*. As these places go they've done their best to make it an attractive place, with roses, lawns and ornamental trees and stonework. It's a far cry from Mont Vésuve, anyway. When you arrive Richard the no-nonsense *concierge* shakes your hand, asks how you are, helps you unload your rubbish into the correct container and even sweeps out your trailer for you. Some people take great pleasure from throwing larger items of rubbish out – indeed, the people of Prague once threw an entire city council out of the town hall window into the river below – and I suspect people go there as much to meet and chat as for the cathartic enjoyment of heaving an old television down into the *encombrants* (general clutter) hopper. I once suggested to Richard that he should recognise the social potential of his *déchetterie* by opening a bar there. For a moment or two he took me seriously. There's a first time for everything, after all.

Montpellier. The big city. It's bitterly cold. We can see a huge bank of snow-laden cloud heading towards us from the direction of Marseilles and the Camargue. We've already seen TV news pictures of Marseilles traffic brought to a halt by a couple of centimetres of slush. The southern *autoroutes* are lined with kilometres of lorries parked nose to tail, corralled by the police against an accident. La Croix Rouge, the Red Cross, moves among the drivers, distributing hot meals and cigarettes. There's a sort of jolly Dunkirk spirit, resignation to enforced idleness. Perishables are hardly at risk in this weather. It's warmer inside the refrigeration units. Is this what we moved to the south of France for?

But never mind that. There's protection of a different sort, and not too much enforced idleness, for *convoyeurs de fonds*, the armoured bullion carriers, though. We've seen TV news pictures of them, too, coursing through the streets of Paris with police and soldiers riding shotgun. It's the same in other big cities, throughout Europe. It's a massive exercise.

They're delivering euros. In Montpellier they've obviously braved snow, black ice, bandits, heists and hold-ups, because they've delivered the goods. In the Post Office, which is wonderfully warm, a pretty girl in a blue smock directs us to the right queue. We wait a few minutes, and presently a counter assistant takes our 100 franc notes and hands us a pack of the first euro coins ever in exchange. €15.24-worth, although when we open the pack there's €15.25 in it. We've made 1 euro-centime on the deal. No notes yet: we have to wait until the official change-over date, January 1st.

All this is happening in mid-December. The government has decided to release euro-coins in advance, to allow people the experience of handling them and to get used to the denominations. We can't spend them until New Year's Day.

We take them home, open the packs and look at them. We feel we're in at a historic moment, and we wish we could share it with our compatriots north of the Channel. They're shiny and new, like foil-wrapped chocolate coins. Some are very small, some are dated 1999, so they've waited some time in the wings. They're all marked with their denomination, of course, but on the other side there's the famous *semeuse*, the girl sower, who featured on the old 1 franc coin. It's the only link with France. They're valid thoughout Europe – at least, in all those member countries of the monetary union. No more changing into escudos, pesetas, guilders, punts, schillings, Uncle Tom deutschmark and all. Wonderful. I'm all for bringing people together, even if it's only to grumble about how poor we are.

* * *

So we've some farewells to make, to all those great Frenchmen and Frenchwomen who have accompanied us for so long:

Adieu, Marie Curie, nuclear physicist, on the 500 franc note. I'm sorry we saw so little of each other.

Adieu, Gustave Eiffel, on the 200 franc note: engineer *extraordinaire*, designer not only of the Eiffel Tower but of the railway bridge in our village.

Adieu, Paul Cézanne, impressionist artist, on the 100 franc note.

Adieu, Antoine de St Exupéry, pilot, explorer, author (*The Little Prince*), guardian of the 50 franc note.

But what about Claude Debussy, composer and connoisseur of fine women, gracing the 20 franc note? To you it's not *adieu*, with its sense of finality, but a*u revoir*. I can just about afford to hang on to you and use you as a sentimental bookmark. I expect you would have enjoyed the following story, one that the lovely Louise came up with.

* * *

The old francs died one by one and went to heaven. First to tap at the pearly gates was the 500 franc note: God looked it up and down, sniffed disapprovingly and said 'OK, you, there's your place in eternity, over there, right at the back.' The 500 franc note shuffled off grudgingly, thinking it deserved better treatment than this.

Next the 200 franc note appeared through the gates. 'Right', said God, 'I've got a place for you, over there, just in front of the 500 franc note. Off you go.'

The 100 franc note was told to go and stand just in front of the 200 franc note, the 50 in front of the 100, the 20 in front of the 50.

The coins started to appear. The 10 franc piece found its place just in front of the 20 franc note, the 5 franc piece in front of the 10, and so on with the 2 franc, the 1 franc, the 50 centimes, the 20, the 10.

Finally the tiny 5 centime piece appeared. The trumpets rang out, angelic choirs sang, the heavenly host cheered and God said 'Good to see you, old friend. Come and sit at my right hand.'

There was immediate protest from the 500 franc note, outraged at this blatant favouritism. 'Pipe down, you,' God said. 'When you were on earth, I don't ever remember seeing you in church, but this little chap and his like turned up faithfully, Sunday after Sunday.'

The Fable of the Wasp and the Spider

There's an unexpected duel going on inside our letter-box. You wouldn't have thought it, just looking at it from the outside, but inside its placid green exterior there's goodness knows what Gallic mayhem and brouhaha going on . . .

The spider got there first, maybe over-expectant of fat juicy flies blundering in from the spring sunshine through the letter-flap. Second to arrive was an over-wintering wasp, looking for somewhere quiet and sheltered to build its nest. I should have got rid of them both, of course, but it occurred to me that just as the Romans tried to

44

foretell the future by counting birds in the sky or examining chicken entrails, so the denizens of our letter-box, if left to themselves, might foretell the result of the French presidential elections. In any case we generally buy our chickens oven-ready.

Anyway, the inner life of the letter-box was rudely shaken the other day with two massive sheaves of papers thrust inside, one for each of us. They were election manifestos, 4-page addresses from each of the 16 candidates. Folded inside were 16 voting slips, each printed with a wannabe-President's name. We looked at them closely round the breakfast table. Very curious. As non-French citizens we can't vote in these elections. Local elections, yes, and European ones too, but the Chambre des Députés and the President have to assume office without our suffrage. Why had they been delivered, then? We could only assume that *La Poste* in the village had been told to stuff them into every letter-box regardless of spiders, wasps or the electoral status of the householder.

But there they all were. The front-runners (as it seemed), the retiring President Jacques Chirac, the retiring Prime Minister Lionel Jospin: scarred veterans of presidential elections like Robert Hue, the teddy-bear-like communist leader; the untiring candidate for The Workers' Struggle, simply known as Arlette, and the sinister Jean-Marie Le Pen, accompanied on the National Front campaign trail by shaven-headed heavies, his election rallies always slightly reminiscent of Nuremburg 1936. A fair sprinkling of left-wing hopefuls, including a smiling Revolutionary Communist postman (not ours), and a maverick or two including Jean Saint-Josse, who stands for a party called *Chasse, Pêche, Nature, Tradition* (CPNT), a deepest-France affiliation of hunters, shooters and fishers who don't want their rural conservatism mucked about by Brussels.

* * *

French presidential elections take place in two stages a fortnight apart. The two front runners from Stage 1 slog it out in Stage 2. It's not a bad system: everyone has their chance, the mavericks and no-hopers are eliminated, protest votes are registered, two serious candidates emerge. Or that's the theory.

We switched on the television in the evening of Stage 1. Chirac and Jospin would emerge, undoubtedly. All the polls forecast it. No other result was possible. Centre left versus centre right. Same old contest. *Plus ça change*. . . but at 8pm the blow fell, and all France rocked. You could probably have heard the gasp of disbelief and consternation. Jospin's vote had melted away, scattered like birdseed among the other socialist candidates and especially among the 11 million – out of an electorate of 41 million – who hadn't bothered to vote.

The unthinkable had happened. Le Pen was in the final. His vote had increased slightly, a percentage point or two up on previous presidential elections, enough to draw attention to the problems of law and order, unemployment and immigration that worry so many French people but not enough to suggest that a crushing majority wanted a jackboot régime.

At last, French politics were getting interesting. Impromptu anti-National Front demonstrations materialised in the cities. Uncomprehending, tearful Jospin supporters poured on to the streets. Disappointed Communists and Trotskyites urged their followers to block Le Pen at all costs in the second round, which was tantamount to telling them to vote for Chirac. Things had taken a strange turn.

* * *

In the morning, after a night troubled by thoughts of what might happen if Le Pen got in and really did send all foreigners home, or somewhere else anyway, I went down to the *mairie*, where the local results were pinned up on the door. There are only about 400 electors in the village, but the results weren't wholly typical of the rest of France:

46

Jospin	67
Saint-Josse	58
Le Pen	48
Chirac	46

– and the rest came in nowhere, unless you count Abstentions and Spoilt Papers 108 as a positive result.

* * *

Everyone knows now that in the final result Chirac swept to victory, of course, but at this point between the first and second rounds reading the auguries wasn't easy. Things took a pretty dramatic turn in our letter-box: I looked in one morning and found a lifeless black-and-yellow cadaver lying at the bottom. The wasp was no more, the spider reigned unchallenged. What did this betoken? In Classical times oracles were notoriously ambiguous. Was Chirac, a man with at least a question-mark over some financial features of his past – was Chirac the wasp or the spider?

Somebody else hadn't found the solution, either. At one of the countless anti-National Front demos held all over France, among the many waving placards we read VOTEZ ESCROC, PAS FACHO. Vote Crook, not Fascist. Maybe it's just as well we don't have the vote.

A Game of Soldiers

Whoever won the presidential election was guaranteed the best seat in the house for the traditional July 14th military parade. The day, *la fête nationale*, is a national holiday to commemorate the 1789 fall of the Bastille, the Paris prison/fortress symbolic of royalist rule, broken into by a revolutionary mob, while the annual march-past of French armed

47

forces is supposed to affirm their allegiance to the French nation in the person of the President. I too, a closet sucker for pomp and circumstance, usually procure for myself the best seat in the house in front of the television to gawp at the endless battalions swinging down the Champs Elysées to salute the President.

It's much the same every year, the usual ballet of military parades, endless spruce and spiffed up battalions: sword-swinging cadets from the military academies, platoons from serving units, the jingling harness of the Garde Républicaine, police motor-cycle units, trundling tank transporters and armoured personnel carriers, the Paris Fire Brigade, a fly-past from what the French call *l'armée de l'air*. There are usually topical guests: there have been cadets from West Point and a NYFD fire engine to mark a special Franco-American empathy with 9/11; a company of the Grenadier Guards, the band of the Royal Marines and the King's Troop, Royal Artillery to mark the centenary of the Entente Cordiale; another highlight has been a marching band from Brazil, rich in percussion.

The climax for spit-and-polish fans comes when the marching units have finished and the armoured car and artillery motorcade is about to start. It's very dramatic: the bands stop, a hush falls, and in the distance, several blocks down the Champs Elysées, a different music starts, at a slower pace, 90 to the minute for military march experts: it's the Foreign Legion, magnificently bearded, in white *képis*, scarlet epaulettes and immaculately pressed khaki drill, marching ponderously at what they call the *pas de sable*, the sand-pace, as though they were stomping determinedly across the Sahara to relieve Fort Zinderneuf from besieging Touaregs. They bring their own music with them, led by staff-twirling bandmasters. No French citizen can serve in the Legion's ranks, of course, and we're told that the band – a very professional one – is made up of musicians from eastern Europe, where the musical training is exacting but jobs non-existent. Signing on with the French Foreign Legion is one way out of this *impasse*.

* * *

I once had a curious encounter with the Foreign Legion. Driving along the narrow Route de Narbonne in Labastide Rouairoux some years ago, I edged on to the pavement to let a camouflage-green military bus past. *4ème Régiment, Légion Etrangère,* the destination board said. The fabled Foreign Legion!

My concepts and notions of the Foreign Legion had been formed many years before, generally on Wednesdays in the 1950s when the week's issue of *Eagle* came out. Men and boys of my generation will recognise, some blinking back tears of nostalgia, that *Eagle* for main course and *Beano* and *Dandy* for afters offered an unparallelled diet of hidden curriculum. In those heady days of innocence the upper centrefold of *Eagle* featured a cutaway drawing of some topical piece of engineering like the De Havilland Comet or HMS Ark Royal, while the lower part was occupied by *Luck of the Legion.* This strip cartoon unfolded the Saharan adventures of Sergeant 'Tough' Luck and his Foreign Legion sidekicks Corporal Trenet and Private Bimberg, a fatso noted for exclaiming *Sacré bleu!* and *Nom d'une pipe!* – expressions which have a certain antique innocence to them, like O Bother! or Great Scott! which I don't expect you hear very often, say, in the Brigade of Gurkhas, maybe the UK's nearest approach to the Foreign Legion. Another Bimberg favourite was *Sapristi!* I came across this expletive, which I thought mild enough, in a song about *clafoutis,* a kind of cherry pie that we'll meet in more detail later on, which I taught once to a class of children in St Pons. Madame la Directrice disapproved: while it wasn't deeply offensive, it wasn't very polite, nor was it really acceptable in a Catholic primary school. She suggested a harmless alternative, and henceforth the kids sang the anodyne *'clafoutis si joli'* instead of *'clafoutis sapristi'.* So maybe there was a barrack-room edge occasionally to Private Bimberg's tongue.

Anyway, as the bus passed, my eyes strayed upwards for a glimpse of a latter-day Sergeant 'Tough' Luck in sun-bleached, sweat-stained *képi* and neckcloth. I looked up in vain. No *légionnaires.* The bus was

49

full of glum women, overdressed and heavily made up. They had the torpid air of the night shift about to clock on, much to the corporal relief of Fort Zinderneuf, or wherever the 4th Regiment was stationed. There was never anything like this in *Eagle*. *Sapristi!* as Bimberg would have said. Or would he have come out with what the French, uncharacteristically euphemistic, sometimes call *le mot de Cambronne*, Cambronne's word?

* * *

A recent July 14th parade included a pageant to celebrate the bicentenary of La Légion d'Honneur, the honorific order instituted by Napoleon. Young people paraded irregular shapes of stretched coloured cloth which, when seen from the Presidential dais, eventually formed themselves into a giant gold medal, clasp and ribbon of the Légion d'Honneur. To give a sense of history, each jigsaw piece was accompanied by a small group in the military or civilian dress of the period.

So among others we had Chasseurs Alpins from 1940, *poilus* from the First World War, cavalrymen from the Crimea, and dating back to 1802, two fearsomely moustached grenadiers of Napoleon's Old Guard, blue tunics, white crossed shoulder-straps, bearskin with red cockade.

At Waterloo Napoleon, out of sorts that day – some say through having dosed himself with laudanum, others because of his piles – neglected to deploy his Old Guard, so they stood about all day doing nothing while their general, Cambronne, fretted and fumed. At the end of the day the victorious British and Prussians called on the Old Guard, standing firm but inactive while the remnants of the French army melted away, to surrender.

Merde! (Shit!) was the answer from the ranks, or maybe from Cambronne himself. At least, according to some. Others claim that what Cambronne really said was *La Garde meurt et ne se rend pas*, the Guard dies rather than surrender, and I suppose it could just be said that the word *meurt* sounds something like *merde*. To have a swearword named after you must be almost as great an honour as being awarded the Légion d'Honneur. And about as unlikely as Madame la Directrice coming out with *le mot de Cambronne*.

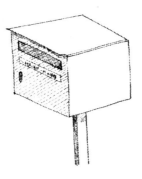

TRADESMEN'S ENTRANCE

A Clash of Symbols

Ah, the Languedoc! Northerners say, when we tell them where we live. Their eyes film over as they drift off into agreeable holiday visions of sunshine, vineyards, shady olive groves, drowsy scents of wild thyme, the constant summer song of cricket and cicada (which really sounds like your neighbours and all their children playing maracas from dawn to dusk) and many other things that you could turn into tourist office slogans: *Languedoc, Land of Wine, Women and Song* . . . *Languedoc, Land of Fine Food and Farniente* . . . *Languedoc: Don't Forget the Ambre Solaire* . . . and in any competition (first prize: a pair of maracas) to find the most original slogan I don't expect *Languedoc: Land of Tumbledown Sheds* would trouble the judges much.

But it's true. Per square kilometre there must be more decrepit, multi-cobwebbed, junk-ridden, bat-haunted, lizard-running hovels than anywhere else in Europe. We bought one once, in the hamlet of

Mousse le Grieux, intending to convert it into part of a house. The first citizen and prime shed-owner of Mousse le Grieux was René Bosc. His hovel was a strong challenger in the Languedoc Tumbledown Shed stakes: its rocky – in both senses – structure was stabilised only by a monumental heap of chicken manure in one corner. Its walls bulged ominously inwards and Pythagoras, if asked to define its shape, would have come out with whatever the Greek is for an irregular trapezoid.

There were two clinchers that guaranteed the absolute genuineness of this decrepit drum. Slung from a wormy chestnut beam, masked from view by the cobwebs, was what René called *un moine*, a monk. We'd come across *moines*, symbols of a bygone age and a hardier race, before. During a very early house-hunting expedition we'd taken one home to Scotland, convinced that antique and curio dealers would fall over themselves to fork out for such a recherché artefact: had we stumbled across the very article that no style-conscious household could be without? About 120cm long and 30cm wide, lightly constructed of wood, it tapered at both ends to form a shape roughly reminiscent of a sort of square-cut cigar. In the middle was a square metal plate. If I'd asked René, who loved his *blague*, i.e. joke, he would have tried to convince me that it was a sledge, or a spare wing section of the very aircraft that carried Louis Blériot across the Channel in 1909, but I'd met *moines* before, in the outhouses of the half-village we nearly bought some years before. They're the Midi equivalent of the warming-pan: on cold nights you took a hot brick or stone out of the ashes of the fire, wrapped it in flannel, put it on the central metal plate of the *moine* and slid the whole contraption between the sheets. I tried it once. As a bed-warmer of its day the 'monk' must have been very efficient, second to none, as you might say.

The other clincher was more sinister. Hanging from a nail was a World War II helmet, unmistakeably German, a relic of wartime occupation. We asked René where it had come from. From a sudden upward movement of his hand with fingers outspread at the same time as he lowered his head, lips pursed – try it, if you like: you'll feel much better – we understood that he didn't know, and didn't much care, but it was very useful when slung from one arm for scattering fertiliser grains or slug pellets over his vegetable garden.

When the chicken manure had been carted away and Christian Cabrol the builder had started on the project it needed the merest nudge from his Bobcat mini-digger to demolish what had been René's shed. Great was the fall thereof, and maybe buried in the hard core beneath what was to become the new entrance hall is a lump of twisted metal that once bore the symbols of the 2nd SS Panzer Division. At any rate, the helmet disappeared without trace. I don't expect that we shall ever know what became of the head inside it, either.

Shortly after the collapse of René's shed another relic of turbulent times came to light. Clearing away the rubble Christian's son Fabien, an athletic lad who plays *treize* (i.e. 13, meaning Rugby League) for a village on the Canal du Midi called Homps, uncovered a stainless steel spoon, as bright, shining and solid as on the day some 60 years ago when an unknown German soldier dropped it; a reasonably safe conjecture because engraved on the handle were the symbolised wings of the Wehrmacht and, between them, a swastika. *C'est un trophée!* Christian exclaimed, and Fabien played finders keepers and took the spoon home with him.

As for me, I wondered how it had got there. Had some lowly Teutonic soldier, who like most of us at heart wished no harm to anyone, sat himself in the doorway of René's shed, his dusty boots dull in the midday sun, spooning sauerkraut and dumplings out of his mess-tin, prematurely counting his lucky stars that he'd been posted to the South of France instead of the Russian front? Was there a sudden crack of a Resistance rifle from the rocks and trees across the valley? Had his unfastened helmet . . .? – but you can fill in the rest yourself. *Et in Arcadia ego . . .*

We'd been worried about the state of our roof timbers for some time. To the naked eye, shaded against the sun, looking upwards to the green-painted beam-ends, soffits and weatherboarding, their days were numbered, in single figures. We looked about for a reputable builder to replace them. Christian Cabrol asked to be excused. He'd recently moved to Carcassonne, and the daily two-hour journey up and over the Minervois to Olargues via his depot at Félines Minervois was just too much for his old lorry, Fabien the prop forward and himself. Besides, he had more work than he knew what to do with. As it was he spent what was left of his evenings fending off exasperated clients with untenable promises and if he took this job they'd all look elsewhere, and as for his little business, it would be *bonsoir Barbara*, a curious expression he sometimes used meaning it would be all up, curtains, the end, RIP.

At that moment many French households found themselves gripped by a panic all the more devouring because nobody could admit to it. The euro was due in a few weeks' time: there would soon be a big question-mark over all those legendary tax-shy francs hoarded in uncounted mattresses and hearthside hidey-holes, a traditional home banking system the French call *bas de laine*, woollen stockings. (This is a term that puzzled me greatly when I first heard it: the speaker had a cold, and I understood *madeleine*, which is a kind of cake. One had heard of sixpences in the Christmas pudding, but . . .)

Solutions were few. Put it on deposit? The banks are obliged to declare deposits above a certain modest level to the tax authorities.

Just hang on to it? Not really a good idea: the franc would cease to be legal tender in due course.

Translate it into something else, some other commodity that would keep its value? This seemed to be the preferred option. At any rate, in the months before the euro came in there was a curiously inexplicable cash spending frenzy, mostly benefitting jewellers and jobbing builders. The path was still stony: jewellers were obliged to charge VAT, at that time 20.6%, but if you tried extra hard you might just find a builder who would take cash for converting the loft or retiling the *salon* floor, cash with a nod and a wink and a shake of the hand, no income tax, no VAT and the poor old taxman gnashing his fangs.

So we were lucky to find M. Mosé, a builder everyone spoke well of, with a gap in his forward planning, and by this time particularly anxious to mix some legitimate business with the mattress emptyings. Legitimate business? Why, yes: without a quote and a matching bill clearly showing VAT paid, no insurance company would look at any claim. Worse, you couldn't set the cost of improvements against capital gains tax if ever you came to sell the property. If they don't get you one way, they'll get you in another. That's the genius of – but never mind all that: on the appointed day M. Mosé and his merry *maçons* turned up, put up some stout scaffolding, stripped the edge tiles and started on the crumbling, worm-eaten eaves. It wasn't hard. Lumps and flakes of green-painted woodwork came away at the first stroke of the pick and showered down on to the *terrasse* below.

Presently an anxious-looking M. Mosé tapped at the door, accompanied by his foreman, a slender, wiry woman called Nadine. He didn't want to worry us, but did we know our roof timbers were infested with capricorns? He'd cut an inspection hole through the *voliges* (the roof boarding beneath the tiles) and he could practically hear the larvae wishing each other *bon appetit.* Some of the rafters were so chewed that a fall of snow would cause immediate and catastrophic collapse.

Capricorns? This was something new. We'd never heard of them, except as a birth-sign. Ah, they were very interesting, capricorns, M. Mosé said, understandably warming to something that put thousands of francs into his pocket every year. They came from the United States, he said. They'd first crossed the Atlantic in 1944, at the time of the

Normandy landings, as grubs in wooden munition boxes and armament cases, which the allied armies abandoned as soon as they were opened. In the wake of the allied advance a tide of temporary war-damage repairs as well as countless lean-tos, sheds, outdoor loos and especially hen-houses swept through Normandy. As the troops advanced, so did the capricorns. And now here they were, sixty years on, in the deep south.

So we sighed deeply, took a deep breath and agreed to have the whole roof replaced, our Christmas present for this year and many years to follow. Hardly had M. Mosé gone away to price it than one of the storms which occasionally ravage the Languedoc tugged and bit at the tarpaulins and tore us from sleep as the heavens opened, and far from the capricorns doing their worst it was the aquarians that had it in for us. We passed a wet night inside and out.

* * *

With a virgin roof in *tuiles vieillies* (pre-aged tiles, factory-mottled to give the appearance of great age) M. Mosé arranged for the infected timbers to be taken up to Mont Vésuve for burning, the only sure way to combat the spread of capricorns.

The working week's last lorry-load left at about 4.30 on a Friday afternoon, leaving on the front lawn a few final planks and beams, showing green where they'd once formed the eaves, to be disposed of the following Monday. At 5.00 a small van passed coming down from Mont Vésuve, its roof-rack grotesquely overladen with newly-dumped planks and beams. Green-tipped, of course. Some dump-scavenger hadn't wasted his time. Before nightfall someone else knocked at the door. He was desolated to disturb us, he said, but he was building a new hen-house. If nobody wanted those old planks there on the grass, could he perhaps . . . ?

Then we found a stash of boards under the box hedge, neatly camouflaged with their dark green paint. We raised an eyebrow: what were they doing there? Oh, said Stan – an unlikely name for a French builder, you might think: his brother's called Oliver, apparently. This explains as much as it defies explanation – Oh, said Stan, they're mine. You don't mind, do you? I'm building a hen-house, you see.

* * *

Were we vouchsafed a premonition of all this? Some while before all this business with new money and new roofs we opened a tin of chicken-based cat-food and dished some out for our feed-on-demand cats Pinot and Merlot. They're French cats, but that doesn't stop them being as sniffy as cats from anywhere else about what they eat. They left quite a lot of their *poulet aux légumes*, which I suppose you could translate as chicken 'n' veg.

But they had reason to turn their noses up. When we looked closely in their bowl, the green leavings that we'd supposed were bits of haricot beans turned out to be chips of green-painted wood. More lurked in the tin. We could only suppose that into the giant maw of the pet food processor had gone everything, chicken carcases, neck, crop, bones and hen-house too.

At least this happened before work started on our new roof. I hereby abdicate all responsibility for the onward march of capricorns.

A Little Custom

The voice on the telphone said *Venez déjeuner, monsieur.* Come for breakfast. We like to finish each job with a meal. It's just a little custom we have. Please join us. We'll expect you about 7.30. *D'accord?*

I replied *Oui, d'accord, merci* and put the phone down, wondering what I was letting myself in for. Breakfast? I couldn't remember ever having received an invitation to breakfast before. I noted the time, place and date with a publicity pen my breakfast host had given me, one of several he had showered on me in a sudden burst of generosity. A kindly nature, evidently. It it wasn't breakfasts he was giving away, it was pens. The barrel was decorated with seagulls, birds we never see in this part of France, flying about or perched morosely on mooring posts, on either side of the inscription, *Bernard Julié, Parqueteur* and his telephone number in Mazamet, a town about 20 minutes down the valley from Labastide.

A *parqueteur* is a floor specialist. M. Julié had been contracted to sand, seal and vitrify the wooden floors of a house belonging to some friends while they were away. I'm not sure that 'vitrify' exists in English, at least not in the sense I'm looking for, but it's the most convenient translation I can come up with for *vitrifier*, meaning to spread evenly over the floor a noisome substance looking like treacle which hardens into a glossy non-slip surface like a school gym at the start of term. So 'vitrify' it is: why use thirty words when one will do? The realisation comes to me that all this cod narrative, taking about a hundred words to explain how to reduce thirty words to one, is in itself a metaphor for the science of economics.

However, I was really much more concerned about an invitation to breakfast, particularly a French breakfast. No Frenchman is proud of his breakfast. If they exist at all French breakfasts tend to be furtive, hurried, hole-and-corner affairs, a rusk or a croissant dunked in a cereal-sized bowl of chocolate or coffee, not the sort of thing you invite guests to. There's a growing market for children's breakfast cereals, which have an unfortunate tendency to be given names that make British kids on holiday in France roll about the supermarket aisles helpless with laughter, names like *Plopsies* or *Jobiz*. I was fairly certain that this sort of thing wouldn't be on M. Julié's menu, but all the same I took the precaution of stoking up with porridge, tea, toast and marmalade, and I set off, expecting to be back well in time for mid-morning coffee.

It had been arranged that I should lock up when M. Julié and his henchman Denis had finished. The job had come to an end the day before, the final drying had taken place overnight, and when I arrived at 7.30 M. Julié had replaced the last of the furniture and was loading his van, a plain white Citroën van disappointingly free of seagulls. I hardly dared set foot on his beautiful floor, which gleamed and shone like burnished copper; not a speck of dust, a smear, a smudge, a ragged edge anywhere. A truly professional, perfectionist piece of work. I picked my way from mat to mat to reach the table, completely unprepared for the surprise that was to follow.

We sat down just as the church clock down in the village of Les Verreries de Moussans was striking eight. From the capacious cool-box that French tradesmen take about with them M. Julié produced plates, cutlery, glasses and napkins. A fresh *flûte*, a loaf almost a metre long, lay on the table already. He served the first course, *jambon de montagne*, centimetre-thick slices of upland ham, dark and succulent, a good chew needing something to lubricate it, so the first bottle appeared, a 2-year-old Côtes du Rhone. The French have a habit of half-filling your wineglass and keeping it at that level through frequent toppings-up, so that it's difficult to keep track of how much you've drunk.

The conversation was lively and unflagging. It turned out that Denis, M. Julié's *ouvrier* or assistant, had worked on the North Sea oilrigs for some years. This was a world I was slightly familiar with, having worked in that part of Scotland for many years. Denis knew Aberdeen well, particularly Pittodrie, the Aberdeen football stadium, and recalled the great days when the Dons under Alex Ferguson carried all before them, including the European Cup Winners' Cup, the heady days of *Strashang* and *Arshibal*, and it took me a moment to identify these as Strachan and Archibald. There's always a comfortable feeling when people come out with small-worldisms like this: you don't feel such a stranger, you feel that at heart there's no lack of bridges between people if only they'll take the trouble to look for them. Of course, a glass of wine at 8.30 in the morning helps these lofty visions along tremendously.

And not just one. A second bottle appeared with the *assiette paysanne*, a super-salad of sliced sausage, tomatoes, cucumber, three varieties of lettuce, sliced onion, gherkins, beetroot, a few olives, chick peas, shredded celery, with plenty of bread to wipe up the dressing. Sardines followed, and more bread. Cheese, and more wine. Fruit. Finally coffee, unexpectedly good from a flask, at about 11 o'clock, when I was beginning to feel breathless, if not vitrified. I couldn't have swallowed anything, not even my own words about the direness of ordinary French breakfasts.

We cleared away, consigning the débris and empty bottles to the *poubelle*, the village wheelie-bin. I locked up as promised, thanked them for allowing me to share their little custom, and we shook hands. I knew where I was going: for an unashamed midday snooze. As for M. Julié and Denis, they had other fish to fry. They had another job to start in the afternoon, but meantime they were going home to Mazamet. For lunch. I raised an eyebrow. For *lunch?*

Oui, monsieur, M. Julié said, another little custom . . .

AT THE TROUGH

Chestnut stuffing

When Gilbert (who takes the occasional turn out of his kitchen into these pages) and Claudine were casting about for a name for their restaurant in the village of St Etienne d'Albagnan, they didn't make any concessions to passing British trade: they came up with Le Châtaignon, a word stuffed with pitfalls for Anglo-Saxons. It comes out something like 'sha-tay-nyaw'. The final 'n' is silent for a start, and you can't hear the 'g' either. And what about that circumflex over the first 'a'? It must be for something more than keeping the rain off. Altogether a slippery customer.

'G' and 'a' lead to a little conundrum that I'll come too in a minute, but you might as well look for a circumflex on a hat-stand as find *châtaignon* in the dictionary, although its neighbours *châtaigne* (chestnut) and *châtaignier* (chestnut tree) may give you a clue. In fact it's a specialist word meaning a kiln-dried, peeled and ready-to-eat chestnut.

It's a perfectly suitable name for a restaurant in the valley of the Jaur, where chestnut trees grow dense and autumn dog-walks are as stuck with chestnut spikes as the word *châtaignon* is studded with linguistic pitfalls. At one time chestnuts were a vital mainstay of the local economy, but now there's only one specialist chestnut farmer in the area, Frédéric. He and his wife Almuth are Germans who came to the valley many years ago looking for the good life, and found it rewarding but far from easy. They've spent the best years of their lives slashing, burning, replanting and restoring an old *châtaigneraie* (chestnut orchard) to its former state. It's a crop won only with immense effort: the traditions of chestnut cultivation linger on in the little museums in St Etienne d'Albagnan and Olargues, where you can see all the old tools of the trade, practically armour-plated against the wicked chestnut spikes that stab you as soon as look at you.

So chestnuts often appear on the menu at Le Châtaignon in one guise or another, sometimes as a few drops of liqueur mixed with white wine to make an excellent *kir*, sometimes as bread or *crêpes* made from chestnut flour. Sometimes Gilbert will serve them as a vegetable braised in chicken stock, and very occasionally they turn up as a stuffing. There are plenty of other good things on the menu, and just as well if you don't like chestnuts, but they're obliged to include them prominently for an unusual reason.

Technically Le Châtaignon is *une auberge*, and here we're plunged unwittingly into a sort of protectionism that, on this level, it's difficult to find much to grumble at. You can get round certain official requirements and take advantage of certain tax concessions, always enormously popular in France, by calling your eatery *une auberge* and binding yourself to feature local produce in your menus. It's a good system, at least in theory: it promotes limited-range produce and provides a modest outlet for local farmers and small-time producers, thus sustaining the local economy and maintaining the old traditions.

In St Etienne d'Albagnan the only beneficiary of this scheme is Frédéric, but elsewhere along the valley there are *auberges* serving local fish, seasonal game like venison and wild boar brought in by the village hunt, fruits and vegetables from the market garden down the lane, wild strawberries and honey from the hills and crayfish from the local rock pools, and so it goes on. The Languedoc cuisine has rarely attracted the attention of the Elizabeth Davids (*French Provincial Cooking, An Omelette and a Glass of Wine*) and Jeanne Strangs (*Goose Fat and Garlic*) of this world, but at its best it is very good indeed and is improving fast. Maybe this is due to the blending of local produce with skills, methods and materials from further afield. Indeed, it's curious that some of the leading practitioners of local cuisine are northerners who have settled in the region. Gilbert himself comes from practically within sight of the White Cliffs of Dover.

Sunday lunch in winter is the time to go to Le Châtaignon, on days when the *tramontane* whistles down from the icy heights of the mountains flanking our valley to the north, when you clutch your collar more tightly about your neck, when you yearn for those balmy summer days of T-shirt and shorts, and when you ponder wrily on the poignancy of 'damart' being one of the classical Greek words meaning 'woman'.

That's the time when Gilbert's fire calls loud and clear. He builds it on a hearth 2 metres by 1, with a cast-iron fireback and firedogs supporting metre-long logs of beech or sometimes vine stumps, gnarled and knobbly, slow-grown to release the concentrated heat of the many summers that ripened past vintages. On the spit there'll be a leg of lamb or pork or wild boar, maybe a haunch of venison or even a pair of ducks. Gilbert will be there, wiping his brow against the heat while holding in the flames a *flambadou*, an ash-grey iron implement like an inverted candle-snuffer with a small hole in the apex of the cone. When it's red-hot he fills the cone with basting fat: it melts and catches almost on the instant, spurting a stream of liquid fire over the meat. Magical. You never tasted such meat.

* * *

'G' and 'a'? All right, if you insist, but it's heavy going. Frederick the Great of Prussia once sent an abstruse and practically incomprehensible dinner invitation that he'd made up to his tutor and friend, the French philosopher Voltaire. It looked something like this:

$$\frac{\text{P}}{\text{Venez}} \qquad à \qquad \frac{\text{Ci}}{\text{Sans}}$$

In English this comes out as: 'Venez' under 'P' at 'Sans' under 'Ci', and we aren't much the wiser. Cracking the Enigma was easier. But remembering that -

1. The letter P in French is pronounced 'pay'
2. The French for 'under' is *sous*, which sounds like 'soo'

– you get the following: *Venez sous p à Sans sous ci.*

Put it into regular French and you get: *Venez souper à Sans souci.* Come and dine at Sans Souci. (Sans Souci, meaning free of care, no worries, was the curious name Frederick the Great gave to his palace at Potsdam.) It wasn't really worth the effort, was it?

Voltaire's RSVP was terse: he wrote 'Ga' on the back of the invitation and returned it. History doesn't tell whether Frederick the Great understood it, or whether the fare on offer at Sans Souci measured up to Gilbert's spit-roasts. Here's the explanation:

Capital G in French is called *G grand.*

This sounds the same as *J'ai grand*, I have (a) big . . .

Small, lower-case a can be called *a petit.*

This sounds the same as *appetit*, appetite.

So the whole comes out as *J'ai grand appetit*, I have a big appetite.

It's maybe a good thing that Voltaire has other claims to fame, but it sums up what we feel about Sunday lunch at Le Châtaignon.

Bread of Heaven

Naturally you see signs saying PAIN every day here in the Midi, or anywhere else in France for that matter, in shop windows and outside the baker's. I suppose for people who don't speak much French it's a joke that wears as thin as for French people seeing SALE on shop windows in the UK; perfectly normal to us, but in French *sale* means dirty.

Monsieur Albert, one of the four bakers in Labastide Rouairoux, advertises his wares on a sandwich board which says PIZZA PAIN. If you park outside the *mairie* in Courniou, the next village, two signs in Martine Houlès' village shop line up to read EXTREME PAIN. Ho ho. 'Extrème' is a kind of ice-cream, but that needn't stop you indulging your childish sense of humour.

If you cherish holiday memories of crossing the *pain* threshold – oh goodness, what have got myself into? – into a village *boulangerie* you'll have realised how close it lies to the heart of everyday life in France, and how the art of breadmaking is valued and honoured beyond the imaginings of people bloated with Mother's Pride. They won't have staled, surely, your memories of those magical sensations as you crunched your teeth into the melting crispness of your *baguette*, maybe still slightly warm from the oven? Did you ever wonder why you couldn't buy such heavenly bread in Britain or the USA? Why the so-called French sticks you bought in the supermarket back at home never came up to scratch? Why you could never recapture those wonderful *alfresco* lunches of cheese, a few olives, a sun-warm peach or two, and of course a fresh *baguette*? And maybe a glass of *rouge* to help it down and the day along? When I lived in Scotland, this was the stuff of dreams that helped the winter pass, the Grampian snows to melt and the high road south to call me to the Channel ports and the Midi sun beyond. Nowadays, though, after living in France for half a generation . . .

* * *

Sunday morning, early. Yawn, stretch, rub eyes, peer at watch in pink dawn light. 7 o'clock. Breathe in fresh morning air, a wonderful daily treat after weeks of stifling summer temperatures. Through the open window, a minute or two later, the angelus rings, calling the faithful to prayer and me to think about the morning's bread. 3 strokes, pause. Another 3, another pause. 3 more, a final pause, then 12 quicker strokes.

Scramble into summer kit, shorts, T-shirt, leather sandals bought several years ago from a travelling sandal-maker in St Pons market. Away down the lane to the village. This morning air is something else: it's like the sinus-teasing bubbles in good champagne, it's like the scent of crushed mint, it's like sliding into a bed of crisp new linen, it's like the tingling all-over rinse of an astringent shower-gel. I expect I could go on, but you've got the message, and anyway here we are at the *boulangerie*.

If you ever read *French Leaves: Letters from the Languedoc* you'll recognise Jean-Marie Gosset, the master baker. He's been at work since since 9.30 the previous evening, preparing his trays of loaves with evocative names, *baguettes, flûtes, boules, miches, épis,* everything from the tiny one-person *ficelle* to the weighty *couronne*, large enough to feed the five thousand . . . and croissants. It's M.Gosset's croissants that bring me here every Sunday morning. I don't think the art of croissant-making has ever been completely mastered in the Midi: maybe it's something to do with butter not being a natural ingredient in a land where olive oil reigns supreme. But M.Gosset, an incomer to the village, has brought from his native Belgium the true art, and never did croissants melt in the mouth more seductively than on our Sunday breakfast table.

Argument simmers about the origins of croissants. The word itself means 'crescent', I suppose because that's the general shape croissants have when they come out of the oven. Some say no, no, everyone knows they're called croissants because they came back from the crusades, where of course the badge of Islam was – and still is – the crescent moon. I don't know where M.Gosset stands on this theory. He's proud that his part of Belgium gave birth to Godefroi de Bouillon, a leader of the First Crusade which captured Jerusalem in 1099. It seems obvious to me that croissants really couldn't be any other shape. M.Gosset makes his by wrapping a slab of butter, beaten with a rolling pin to about the size and thickness of a roof tile, in an envelope of a sort of puff pastry dough. He then cuts the wrapped slab into squares, which he rolls up diagonally, fat in the middle and thin at the ends. Before baking he may tweak the ends round a bit to give his croissants their traditional curve, but he doesn't always bother.

* * *

How do I know all this? Last Sunday morning Mme Gosset was on duty, I suppose having got out of bed just as M.Gosset was getting into it, in their tiny *boulangerie* in the village where customers are announced by a stuffed marmot or gopher just inside the door, which wolf-whistles as you come in. (Sometimes she gives the marmot a few days off, and then it's an owl which hoots to greet you.) Mme Gosset served me our croissants, but also gave me an untitled video cassette. Surprised, I asked what it was about. *C'est pas grand' chose*, it's nothing much, she said: it's just about us. So I took it home, not expecting to be much edified by the home videos of a family we only really knew across the shop counter.

It turned out to be fascinating, a little slice of France few tourists would ever penetrate. It featured firstly Mme Gosset's delivery round, threading a tortuous route through all the ancient stone-built hamlets and isolated settlements of this wonderful Languedoc hill country where the concept of fresh daily bread is undiminished. The second part took us into the bakehouse by night to watch the master baker at work. No real secrets betrayed, of course, but sharp insights – as witness the croissants – into a profession at the heart of everyday French life.

Another M.Gosset's specialities is his *fougasse*, a kind of savoury super-bread that's virtually a meal in itself and is very popular here as a snack or nibble as well as a worthy accompaniment to something more substantial. The video showed him seething chopped onions in white wine ('they're done when they're the same colour as the wine'), frying up *lardons* (small strips of thick bacon cut across the grain) in their own fat, and then stirring both onions and *lardons* into a dough bound and enriched with olive oil, adding a handful of chopped green olives for good measure. The flat loaf, about the size of a dinner plate, comes out of the oven golden brown, and scored across for ease of breaking into sections. It's perfectly delicious.

With the proliferation of breads, all those white-flour *baguettes*, *flûtes, miches, ficelles* and *épis*, the choice is much greater than it used to be. M.Gosset is also prepared to experiment, a bold step in as traditional a village as Olargues. He finds shelf-room for *pain bio* (biological bread, made from insecticide- and nitrate-free cereals), *pain 5 céréales* (a delicious blend of wheat, rye, oats, barley and rice flours) *pain au son* (with bran) and whatever else takes his, or his miller's, fancy. Our once indispensable daily *baguette* has been ousted by M.Gosset's *pain de Somail*, a wholewheat bread, moist and firm and long-lived, in a rectangular shape which means – luxury of luxuries! – that you can toast it, and there's nothing like the waste you get with *baguette*-type loaves, which stale very quickly.

That's not to say that the *baguette* is dying out. Certainly not. All the same, if you're dreaming, as we once did, of those summer holiday *alfresco* lunches and salivating in anticipation of your daily *baguette*, let's hope you're not too late. Non-availability could cause you some pain. Extreme pain, even.

Feed me till I want no more

They're like a thread of pearls, the restaurants along the valley. I suppose you could start at one end and work your way along to the other, sampling *un plat*, a course, at each. Like a pub-crawl, you say? Goodness, no! Nothing so vulgar. Whatever gave you that idea? Oh, grub-crawl is what you said? Sorry, I must have mis-heard you. No, we're a rung or two up the refinement ladder: you see, eating out is so dear to most French people – and to their expat guests – that I can only liken it to an ongoing religious experience. Admittedly I'm writing this on a Sunday morning, when my thoughts should be on the realms of light above rather than the gnashing of teeth below, as the 19th century wit, bon viveur and clergyman Sidney Smith once observed at somebody's table. All I can say in my defence is that whenever I leave one of the valley restaurants I feel warm and comfortable, at ease with myself and glowing with an immense benevolence to everyone else in the world. I'm afraid this generous feeling is all too short-lived and needs constant re-stoking.

There are far too many shrines to goodwill through greed along the valley to visit all in one evening. I suppose if you wanted to spice up an already pretty toothsome prospect you could devise a board game, where restaurants to be visited and the dishes to be drooled over depend on the throw of dice, but it's probably easier to take a taxi: you can savour different courses in a variety of restaurants.

Lacabarède, a village a few kilometres downstream from Labastide Rouairoux, hasn't got very much going for it, like several other towns and villages along the valley of the Thoré which once depended on a wool trade which has now passed elsewhere. But in the square, opposite a lurid crucifix, is l'Oustalet, Occitan for the little hostelry. It's a family concern, a homely village bar and restaurant, an unpretentious temple to provincial cooking. When we go in Claude

Renard, whom we'll meet again later on, gets up from helping his youngest daughter Solenne with her homework (she was learning *Rock Around the Clock* to help her with her English numbers on one occasion) and welcomes us in English with a hint of American to it. He ushers us to a table by the log fire, where a cat lies stretched out beside a bowl of roasted chestnuts. Sébastien, his trainee-waiter son, appears with our *entrée*, our starter, what he calls *une assiette paysanne*, a peasant plate, and before you smirk it's as well to remember that France is the one country in the world where 'peasant', far from being an insult, is a term of commendation and even of envy. But never mind all that, here are our plates loaded with mountain ham, slices of various kinds of sausage and white pudding, with gherkins, butter, olives, grated carrot and vinaigrette dressing, together with a basket of crisp-crusted bread. It's sincere, simple, unsophisticated and perfectly delicious. It's not expensive, either, but then this isn't a place where a summer influx of tourists pushes prices up.

Sébastian betrays his father's training in wishing us *'ave a nice meal, Sir.* Well, it is a nice meal, a meal in itself, and when we have finished Mme Renard, always anxious for a chat, appears wiping her hands on an apron stained with the juices from her wondrous kitchen. Away so soon? she says. Are we not waiting for her inspired *panaché de volailles sauce diable*, her ambrosial confection of duck and guinea-fowl in a sauce of cream and chicken stock, slightly thickened, lightly peppered and laced with armagnac? We have to apologize for not staying longer, but the next place calls.

* * *

All restaurants have their own character, and l'Esclop has its fair share, at least. It's a one-off place, not much more than a shack with a shady *terrasse* beside it, on one side of the road that runs through the village of Prémian, eastwards from Lacabarède and over the Col de la Fenille, through St Pons and along the valley of the Jaur. L'Esclop is Occitan for The Clog. I don't know why so many local eateries cling to Occitan names. Maybe they evoke the traditional qualities and values to be found there. There's certainly a traditional quality of Gallic logic to be had, and for free: French restaurants are supposed to be fairly divided into smoking and non-smoking areas. When you ask Michel Maurin the proprietor where his smoke-free zone is, he points outside to the *terrasse*. The virtually permanent school of *manille* players installed beside the bar glance at the rain outside and smile behind their hands of cards, untroubled inside their smoke screen.

The kitchen, unusually, is on the other side of the road. Hubert Barthès, the popular and efficient *maire* of Prémian, has seen to it that there's a pedestrian crossing between kitchen and restaurant. Given the usual French attitude to pedestrian crossings, i.e. to treat them as acceleration zones, it's not surprising that Nicole Maurin keeps a figure as trim as you might expect from constant traffic-dodging with laden trays, one of which maybe carries our fish course, one of l'Esclop's specialities, *moules marinière*.

She brings them in an immense steaming vat which she puts in the middle of the table, and we ladle out clunking helpings as required. There's something enormously satisfying about getting outside a plateful of mussels steamed in their own juice with some white wine, chopped onion, garlic and a knoblet of butter added. It can be a messy business: the only efficient way to eat them is to select a medium-sized mussel, prise out the orangey-yellow shellfish with a fork, and then use the double shell, which still has some elasticity in the hinge, as a pair of pincers with which to eat the rest. A chilled dry white wine is an indispensable accompaniment: in one of those perfect partnerships that a diverse region will occasionally throw up, the Mediterranean wine producers just along the coast from the Bassin de Thau, where most of our shellfish come from, market a wine called Picpoul de Pinet. Unexceptional in itself, it has a particular and joyous empathy with shellfish. It's a sad moment when the last mussel has disappeared from the bottom of Nicole's vat. Unashamedly we ladle out the remaining liquor, congratulate ourselves and Nicole on a job well done. We manage to resist her urgings to stay for steak and chips, followed by *colonel*, a deadly dessert of lemon sorbet sprinkled with orange zest swimming in vodka. We settle up and head off down the road to Olargues in the taxi. The ten-minute journey just gives us time to set the scene.

* * *

It takes extra helpings of courage and ingenuity to convert an old Citroën garage into a restaurant. For many years M. Planès had run his repair shop in a solidly built and capacious shed, the sort of thing the French call *un hangar*, with a garage yard alongside complete with inspection pit. It's unlikely that he or any of his mechanics took much time off from fitting new exhausts or cannibalising the wrecks in the yard for spare parts to admire the view, but then when you live all day and every day in a situation of great beauty you tend not to give it a second glance; not that you could see much anyway through the dust and spiders' webs of the repair shop windows. The site looks down to the river Jaur and across and up to the hallmark view of Olargues, honey-toned tumbles of village houses spreading down from the elegant medieval bell tower on the top of its bluff, as though they'd been carved out of a prehistoric lava flow. As if this wasn't feast enough, the Pont du Diable, the Devil's Bridge, frames the picture to the left, linking the old village with the main road and debouching beside a run-down riverside tenement, long on the market. In due course M. Planès built himself a much more extensive garage, bright with stainless steel and flags, on the outskirts of the village and put his former premises up for sale.

As anyone who has ever put property on the French market knows, it only needs the right person at the right time and PAF! the roller coaster of *compromis de vente, prêts immobiliers, mandats de procuration* and *actes authentiques*, crewed by *agents immobiliers* and *notaires*, is set to trundle down the rails, lurching uneasily from side to side and leaving you clutching nervously at your vitals. The r.p. at 'the r.t. occurred in the form of Joan and Anders Bøgeskov, who stopped on their way through Olargues one Sunday morning, came, saw and were conquered, as much by the fare on offer as by the spine-tingling realisation that here, after a quarter of a century of searching, they'd found what they were looking for. From her late teenage years Joan dreamed of owning a place where the summer sun shone for longer than it did in her native Denmark, a retreat, a haven, an ivory tower, even, where writers, composers and artists could stay and ply their thoughts, pens or brushes without interruption and with all found. Anders, the dreamer's assistant, stood by stolidly while the vision of the ivory tower shimmered through the run-down tenement. In a lather of excitement they rang the estate agent then and there, Sunday morning or not, and the following conversation took place in halting French:

Bøgeskov: That place beside the river, by the old bridge, has anybody bought it?
Estate Agent: I open on Tuesday morning at 9 o'clock.
B.: Could you just tell us if it's still for sale?
E.A.: Tuesday morning at 9 o'clock
B.: Can you possibly give us some idea of how much they're asking for it?
E.A.: Tuesday morning at 9 o'clock.

There was nothing to be got out of this beyond 48 hours' worth of heel-kicking and frustration (48 and a quarter hours, to be exact, as the estate agent, a devotee of *le petit quart d'heure méditerranéen*, didn't turn up until 9.15), but by 9.30 the following Tuesday the place was theirs, or would be when the roller coaster came to a halt a couple of months later. The wily estate agent hinted that M. Planès' garage would shortly be on the market, just the place for an annexe to the ivory tower, a restaurant, maybe?

As they say in Denmark, in for an *øre*, in for a *krone*, if that's what it took to become the new owner, and so the Danes went for broke. Broke is probably *le mot juste*, the correct term. Several months later we were invited, along with the rest of the village, to the inauguration of what they christened Les Fleurs d'Olargues.

* * *

As we arrive night is falling, and Anders is moving between the tables on the *terrasse*, hanging oil-lamps from the vine- and honeysuckle-covered pergolas, his own winter handiwork, which now spread over the old garage yard. We've dismissed the taxi, we can walk home from here. We're shown to a table overlooking the river, sparkling with the lights of the village rising from the far bank. It's like a pantomime set, an Advent calendar, a *grandeur nature* pop-up book. House martins soar and wheel, snapping up the last flies before roosting. The Pont du Diable and the tower shine, golden under floodlights. This place is something else: great romances begin here; new ideas, trembling with their daring, are born here; old horizons are transcended, the poet's eye rolls in fine frenzy. It looks as if the the poet's pen has been at work on the menu:

Paupiette de veau truffée aux olives noires, canneberges séchées et herbes sauvages de montagne, mijotée au vin blanc du pays, avec son mirepoix de légumes méditerranéens, sa galette de pommes rosevalt et son déglaçage au vin.

This is so beautiful that I'm reluctant to attempt a translation, and I find myself thinking, no doubt very irreverently, that there are scriptural passages, and passages in Shakespeare of equal beauty, and I've no idea what they mean and don't much care: it's enough to hear the rolling words caressing my ears. There's more beauty as Louise and Lola, blonde and brunette pride of Denmark, bring forth this offering in a lordly dish, and slowly, deliberately, at our own rhythm, we pay the dish, the chef, luscious Lou and lovely Lo and indeed the whole of

Joan's and Anders' conception the tribute they all deserve: we leave empty plates.

The question of a dessert arises. Suddenly, out of nowhere, warmed into life by these delights, there comes into my mind a stray quote from the journal kept by the Goncourt brothers, as worthy a couple of 19th century writers as ever looked in the mirror: *Entre la mousse au chocolat et la chartreuse Martha se déserra le corsage*, between the chocolate mousse and the Chartreuse [liqueur] Martha loosened her bodice. Full stop. We wonder who Martha was, and what happened next. We look at each other: shall we order a dessert? Or shan't we? Eventually we settle for Joan's incomparable lemon mousse, and take ourselves home. At our age we can only take so much sensuality.

FLORA AND FAUNA

Cherry ripe

Don't ever become a cherry farmer. Not here in the south of France, anyway. It's much too dicey. The locals point to the increasing unreliability of the cherry crop to show how weather patterns are changing, and they may have a point, although I suspect that a really good cherry crop, one that enables you to put the deposit down on a little van, a Renault Express or some such, white as the blossom that paid for it, means that your trees did well while everybody else's were a complete disaster.

There won't be many new vans this year. In March an early spell of peerless, childhood weather brought out the cherry blossom, and for a couple of weeks the area shone with a virginal lustre to delight the heart of painters, poets ('Loveliest of trees, the cherry now Is hung with bloom along the bough') and purveyors of little white vans. But March warmth is what a French teacher of mine used to call *un faux ami*, a false friend: in April, the cruellest month, the *tramontane* blew cold and mortal, the sap and the bees retreated to their winter quarters again, and the blossom perished. Of our early cherries, the reds – although the ripe fruit is nearly black – we may see 1%, if that.

Except on one tree, which has turned out to be unexpectedly proof against *faux amis, tramontanes* and all the rest. A few years ago Esmé, the sister of the President of a sub-Saharan republic, climbed all over it, picking and eating as she went; the highlight of her stay in Olargues with her cousin, who at that time came to look after the house while we were away. I can quite understand the attraction. There's a lot of innocent pleasure to be had from clambering about in cherry trees, slowly filling the plastic bag hung from your forearm. Her tree has never let us down since. Does she know something we don't? *Merci*, Esmé. When we need a little white van, perhaps you'll come and see us again?

* * *

Red cherries, the ones that aren't sent away commercially for jamming or sold at the roadside, are often frozen just as they are. We put them in 500g bags, and when we want to recall those balmy summer days in the depths of winter, we put a little water in the bottom of the pan, pour a bag of cherries in, add a few sweeteners and simmer them for a couple of minutes. White cherries don't freeze well, but as fresh fruit they're a staple ingredient of a dessert called *clafoutis*. It's a sort of cherry pud, although the basic recipe can be adapted for most seasonal fruits. Could you fancy a taste of deepest France in the early summer? I translate from a booklet of cherry recipes, printed on cerise paper, naturally, put together by a local *groupement féminin agricole rural*, the nearest flowery-pinafore-no-nonsense-country-kitchen French equivalent of the Women's Institute. You'll need 750g of cherries, 6 eggs, 80g flour, 0.25 litre milk, 90g sugar, salt. Kirsch. (Aha: it's getting interesting.)

Mix the flour with the eggs and salt. Add a little milk. Beat the mix well to ensure a light batter. Add the rest of the milk little by little, until the mix takes on the consistency of pancake batter. Add the stalked and stoned cherries and the kirsch. Pour into an oven-proof dish and cook in a hot oven for 35 minutes. Sprinkle with the sugar and leave to cool.

Munch your way through that and you may never climb a cherry tree again. Of course you could disregard all this and just drink the kirsch instead.

* * *

It might have been this very recipe that someone once used to produce a *clafoutis* of monster proportions, not in terms of size but of inconvenience and embarrassment. At the village Festival of Choral Music (also called *La Vallée qui Chante* – The Singing Valley) of which I found myself Artistic Director one Whitsun I put my rehearsal baton down, dismissed the orchestra and singers for a couple of hours before the evening concert and started to put the school canteen – our rehearsal room – back to rights. On a table near the door, where the brass had been sitting, was a cloth-wrapped tart or pie, which certainly wasn't there when the rehearsal started. It turned to be a *clafoutis*. It must have belonged to one of the musicians. That 2nd Trumpet had a lean and hungry look . . .

I gathered it up with my music stand, batons and scores, locked up and set off up the street towards the church, the venue for the concert, not really best pleased that the *Directeur Artistique*, about to lead choirs, orchestra and public into the glories of some of the most sublime choral music ever written, should be lumbered with a stray *clafoutis*. The village street was closed to traffic, because they were holding a *Foire à la Brocante*, a bric-à-brac market, under the plane trees, and many stallholders simply spread their wares on the road.

Among the stallholders was Nicole. Put any thoughts of Nicole, the nubile, deep-cleavaged daughter of certain Renault advertisements out of your mind: our Nicole is almost as broad as tall, and doesn't care, with a smile to match her splendid size, sunny disposition and sovereign appetite. Sniffing appreciatively (*mmm! délicieux! J'adore le clafoutis!*), she gently pulled folds of the cloth apart, revealing the firm, warm, cherry-studded flesh beneath; she picked out a cherry between plump thumb and forefinger and popped it into her mouth. No man with the slightest interest in his food can resist this sort of seduction for long: certainly not me, a hopeless devotee of Samuel Pepys' diary declaration 'women and music I cannot but give way to, whatever my business is'. I thrust the *clafoutis* into her hands and legged it for the church.

Later, after the final echoes of Gabriel Fauré's *Cantique de Jean Racine* had died away, one of the tenors asked me if anyone had found a *clafoutis*. He'd put it down somewhere, he couldn't remember where. Oh, I said, guiltily, was it for anyone in particular? No, he answered, it was for anyone who felt hungry. He had more cherries than he knew what to do with. Such a pity to waste them.

I was happy to assure him that it had been very much appreciated. Wonderful, he said. May I have the dish back? It was quite an old one.

Among the many stresses that Klemperer or Toscanini suffered, I don't expect anguished wondering whether Nicole had eaten an entire *clafoutis* and had then sold the dish at her bric-à-brac stall was one of them. But I know how Samuel Pepys felt.

And while we're on the subject of women, music and cherries, *Le Temps des Cerises*, Cherry Time, is a haunting little song that's charmed its way into the French national consciousness ever since a hardened Paris republican and lyricist, Jean-Baptiste Clément, and a musician called Antoine Renard put it together about 140 years ago. It's shot through with a wistful melancholy, the sort of cosy nostalgia that you can wrap round yourself to keep the real world out when they play *Keep the Home Fires Burning* or *Lili Marlene* or *Yesterday* slow and soft on the mouth organ or its big brother, the French *musette* or button accordion. All the same, there's an edge, a sharpness like an unripe cherry to the lyric that doesn't come out in the tune:

'Sing in cherry time,' a loose translation runs, 'and the nightingale and the mocking blackbird will be *en fête*. Spring fever turns the heads of pretty girls, the sun shines in lovers' hearts. Sing in cherry time, and the blackbird will mock you the more.' It goes on to mourn the days of innocence before disappointed love left its scars. Heigh ho.

It caught on in the dark days of the Franco-Prussian war, when the Second Empire fell, and became a sort of anthem of the Paris Commune. Napoleon III, Bonaparte's nephew, escaped to exile in England (to Chislehurst, to be exact, where he enjoyed watching cricket), leaving Paris under siege, starving, and the Commune taking the reins of the city's government, variously heroic or crack-brained according to your political persuasion. There's no mistaking the yearning for happier days. They don't write them like that any more, do they?

In full fig

We returned from a few days away to find our other car bloodily streaked and spattered with red, as though a local Hannibal Lecter or Sweeney Todd had butchered some victim on it while we were away . . . with no time to do more than clear off the grosser dark-red gobbets I drove off to an appointment in Labastide, where I parked just in front of three village worthies sitting on a low wall and idly putting the world to rights. They stared in disbelief at this bloody apparition, witness of who knew what carnage. '*Oh-là-là*', said the first, shaking his head slowly from side to side. '*Oh-là-là là-là*', said the second, and I'm afraid I didn't wait to hear whether the third came out with '*Oh-là-là là-là là-là*' although it's true that each pair of '*là-làs*' intensifies the previous one. You should try it some time, with the emphasis on the second '*là*'. You'll be the envy of your French evening class.

The culprit – but you've guessed, haven't you? – was our fig tree, laden with ripe blood-red fruit which plop and splatter on to the white bodywork parked in the shade below.

* * *

Such a bumper crop of figs couldn't go to waste. They're not that easy to preserve successfully, but most summers we make a spiced fig conserve which keeps us going through the winter and well into the following spring and beyond.

Put 2.25kg figs into a pan, with stalks removed and split in half if you want. Sprinkle them with 115g of bicarbonate of soda. Add just under 2 litres of boiling water to cover the fruit. Leave to stand for 5 minutes, then rinse thoroughly in cold water and drain.

Prepare a syrup by dissolving 1.4kg of sugar in 230cl of water and 230cl of vinegar over low heat. Throw in a cinnamon stick and a handful of whole dried pickling spices.

Boil the figs gently in the syrup for 10 minutes on three consecutive mornings, letting them cool and steep in the syrup between each boiling. If the syrup seems too liquid after the third boiling, allow to boil for longer to reduce to the desired consistency.

Pack into sterilised jars and label. Keep in a cool dry place, and refrigerate after opening. Spiced figs will keep for several years.

Try them with roast *pintade*, i.e. guinea fowl, or *magret de canard* (duck breast). Mmmm! Eat enough and you may discover yourself speaking perfect French, with an irreproachable accent. *Bon appetit!*

* * *

The fig tree, *Ficus carica*, grows everywhere and anywhere here, and the seeds (yes, I know, botanists would call them achenes) are so tiny that they lodge in the most minute cracks and crevices, where if there's any moisture at all they germinate and sprout and in no time there's a small tree growing just where you don't want it. A couple of trees, self-planted many years ago, shade our terrace in summer. We barely need to stretch out an arm to pick and eat sun-warmed ripe figs, a luxury we too often take for granted, particularly when we're witness to one of the most extraordinary cases of what the French call *le mutualisme*, which I suppose you could translate as symbiosis, but it's a closer relationship than that. Fig trees can't reproduce without a certain wasp, *Blastophaga psenes*, and *B.p.* can't reproduce without the fig tree. Indeed, fruit farmers trying to introduce the Mediterranean fig to California in the 19th century failed completely until 1889, when *B.p.* was identified as the missing factor. Identification can't have been easy: fig flowers are hidden inside the green bud which grows to become the fruit when fertilised. The male *B.p.*, measuring all of 2mm, spends its short life entirely inside the fig. The female is a little larger, and has wings. Once fertilised by the male, she emerges though the aperture which the male, perfect gentleman, makes for her, whereupon he dies.

The female – and there may be many – flies off, coated with fig pollen from the interior of the green bud. She finds other green buds in which to lay her eggs, incidentally pollinating the fig flowers inside.

There's food for thought here. Where did all this come from? Can two totally interdependent and utterly different species evolve together? We know fig-leaves featured in the Garden of Eden, if only as a kind of primitive bikini or *cache-sexe*, which supposes that *Ficus carica* and *Blastophaga psenes* had been on the go for some time before Adam and Eve, but then it's notoriously easy to pick holes in the Genesis creation story.

Or were the fig and the wasp created simultaneously in an eternal partnership?

Hard questions. No easy answers. We can only say we don't know. As soon as I settle on my lounger to ponder them, straw hat tilted over my eyes, I fall asleep. But maybe Gilbert has the answer?

In my scholarly innocence I'd never before thought of *la figue*, the humble fig, as having other connotations, but Gilbert (pronounced *zheel-bair*), the right-wing guitarist and *chef de cuisine* from Le Châtaignon, assures me that wherever the fig grows it's considered a metaphor for the female genitals, like – it's my comparison, not Gilbert's – wells or jugs or enclosed gardens in religious symbolism or Renaissance painting. Of course, some people are of a cast of mind to find anything suggestive and it's possible that Gilbert was having me on. Given the choice between a ripe fig and a ripe woman I suspect he would choose – but that's neither here nor there. *Oh-là-là*, as you might say. Or even *Oh-là-là là-là*.

Strictly for the birds

On our rare trips to the United Kingdom we try to leave space in the car for goodies unobtainable here in the south of France, things like Marmite, digestive biscuits, porridge oats – but I shan't go on because someone is bound to grumble that if you choose to live in France you ought to cut the umbilical cord, burn your boats, integrate yourself into the local community and settle down to take the whole French experience on board, although how you can take it on board if you've just burned your boats I'm not sure.

Anyway, there we were in an Essex garden centre one November and it seemed to me that it wouldn't be a bad idea to stuff a vacant space in the car-boot with a few bird feeders and some bags of birdseed and peanuts. These are available in the south of France, to be sure, but not everywhere, and the notion of feeding small birds in winter-time isn't one that's really caught on locally yet. Driving the length of France to get back home I daydreamed about the exotic, multi-coloured southern French birds that would throng the front terrace fig-tree, where I planned to hang the feeders, well out of the way of our cat Pinot. Almost the first thing I did on returning on November 6th was to hang up a seed dispenser.

I wondered at the time if it would be instructive to keep a diary of birds observed and their habits. Instructive? It would have read (we might as well do it in French):

> 6 novembre: rien
> 7 novembre: rien
> 8 novembre: rien
> 9 novembre: rien

– and so on, for days and days. Not a dicky bird, as you might say. I might as well have hung up a pair of socks for all the interest they took. By the end of the month some of the seed had started sprouting, due I suppose to some rain having got in. In fact it wasn't until 13 décembre that a clearly disoriented great tit discovered what I expect they now call Café Campbell. I rushed outside, threw the mildewed and sprouting seed out and refilled with fresh.

All it took was time. They come every day now, the regulars, blue tits, great tits, chaffinches, a robin and some dunnocks. Hardly exotic, in fact almost exactly the same birds as I used to have when I lived in the north of Scotland. Who said something about taking on the whole French experience?

But there's one exception. A neat, busy little bird comes to the seed dispenser, sticks its head in and pulls out seeds which, far from eating, it then throws on to the terrace paving below for the ground feeders, chaffinches and dunnocks. I had to look it up: it's a marsh tit, a very generous little bird, enormously popular with the groundlings that haven't got the hang of seed dispensers. Its largesse clearly reflects its upbringing in the best tradition of socialist, dependency-culture France.

* * *

Even if they're interested it's not easy to discuss bird-watching with the neighbours. The problem lies in translating English variety names into French. I'm reminded of this every time the dawn chorus strikes up through the open summer window: the soloists, like the nightingale just coming off the night shift and the golden oriole tuning up like a clarinet translate easily into *le rossignol* and *le loriot*, but naming the individuals in the chorus of twitterers and cheepers, the Café Campbell regulars, is more difficult.

When I first arrived in France I asked our neighbours in Bardou, the tiny village I first lived in, what this or that little bird was called. My principal informant, Pierrot, was *un paysan* who stumped about the village singing among other snatches of song *Les Petits Oiseaux de la Ferme*, The Little Birds of the Farm, so I supposed he knew all about it. But no, he didn't know, they were just little birds. *Pinsons*, yes, that was what they were, *pinsons*.

This was a bit over-generalised, like saying they were all finches. But there was a way round. Having noticed, for instance, a great tit nesting under the eaves, I could go to Collins' Guide to British Birds for the ornithological Latin: *Parus major*. From the Latin to the French: *mésange charbonnière*. (In case *charbon* suggests 'coal' to you and you have your suspicions, a coal tit is *une mésange noire*.) Faced with this incontrovertible identification, Pierrot would say *Ah oui, peut-être*, ah yes, maybe, and would stump off up to his *potager*, his vegetable garden, to watch his beans grow.

I went to see him once in his house, and a freshly shot thrush was whisked off the table and hidden, I suppose out of respect for my soft northern sensibilities. There weren't more than three bites in it, but I suppose if all you're going to do is eat it you don't really need to know its name. In any language.

* * *

I doubt if even Pierrot would have cast hungry looks at a nightingale, though. They're notoriously invisible, spending most of their time hidden in brakes and thickets and totally spurning the Café Campbell society. I have seen them, but very rarely: for all the volume and variety of its song, the nightingale is about the same size as the robin, a little dun-coloured bird with a creamy underside. They'll steal back – or maybe they've been there all the time? – in the month of May, when suddenly the woods are full of magical music, all night and for much of the day. They'll sing for several weeks, until the nesting season is over and the summer heats begin. We have our fair share, at least: sitting out on the terrace late into the evening we can sometimes count up to six different nightingales, pouring out their nocturnes of *bel canto*. First-time visitors from Britain or the USA, their sensibilities warmed by more wine than they would usually drink on a velvet night in early summer, can become quite dewy-eyed and emotional at the extraordinary beauty of it all: later, around three or four in the morning, they wake up hot, sticky and uncomfortable, wondering how to stop the desperate head-shattering racket in the woods outside.

The BBC in its early days once broadcast a scratchy recording of a famous 'cellist trying to encourage her local nightingale to sing, somewhere in southern England if not in Berkeley Square. There was an element of suspense: would the nightingale oblige, would there be an extraordinary duet, a marriage of art and nature? In my experience nightingales need no encouragement at all, and indeed if the BBC were to come up with some means of shutting them up at unsocial hours it would be well received in certain quarters.

LA CIGALE ayant chanté
Tout l'Esté
Se trouva fort dépourveuë
Quand la Bize fut venuë

– so wrote La Fontaine in the first of his Fables. These Fables appeared in 1668, so the French is a bit old-fashioned. Here's a translation:

The cicada having sung
All the summer
Found herself unprovided for
When the autumn winds came.

The fable goes on to describe how the feckless cicada, having frittered away summer's plenty in singing, is forced to beg for winter food from the industrious and thrifty ant. Despite the cicada's promise to repay everything with interest, the hard-hearted ant refuses to lend anything and advises the cicada to keep warm by dancing: *Eh bien, dansez maintenant,* the ant says, OK, now dance, and, having taken in the moral that we must all be thrifty and make hay while the sun shines we move on to Fable 2, The Fox and the Crow. Not the greatest plot you've ever read.

You can find cicadas in silver and gold, in ceramic, carved from olive wood, as embroidered buttons, in chocolate, in just about any medium you care to mention. But I'd never seen one live until recently. This is strange, given that the song of the cicada is inescapable throughout the summer in the south of France, a continuous maracas-like rattle that starts as soon as the day warms up and which doesn't finish until after nightfall. When eventually it subsides, you can hear the much softer buzz of the cricket and the occasional whispered chirrup of the grasshopper underlying it. Every tree seems to have its resident cicada. They're elusive, all the same: stop beneath a tree to try to locate the singing tenant and it promptly stops. It's a sound that's difficult to pinpoint, too. Move to the left, and it seems to come from your right; move right to locate it, and it shifts back to the left. Very curious.

I found one by chance one August on the slender trunk of an ornamental maple we'd planted in the spring. Maybe this cicada was nearing the end of its short life, but it was still a handsome insect, about 5cm long with a large head, delicately traced wings folded roofwise along its body. It was singing lustily, rattling the plates of its abdomen fit to burst. Always a sucker for novelty and happening to have my mobile with me, I rang my son in the UK to let him hear the music of the Midi direct from our maple tree. What would your reactions have been in similar circumstances? Well, his were just the same.

La Fontaine, a hardened city-dweller, spent most of his life in Paris and never went nearer the Midi than Limoges. I don't expect he was terribly interested in insects. In any case he lifted the story from Aesop, who in turn had it from an eastern oral folk fable. Aesop was careless about the name of the feckless singing creature, or maybe the nearest Greek equivalent to the oriental original was the cicada. The real life of the cicada could have provided material for a truly original fable.

Our cicada doesn't eat, she – we'll make her female out of respect for La Fontaine – only drinks. Liquids are scarce in the often parched Midi, but one invariable source is tree sap. She pierces the bark with her proboscis and sucks away, rattling the tymbals, the plates on her abdomen, the while. The sound or maybe the vibration attracts other thirsty insects, especially ants. They attack her, trying to get her to move away from the water-hole she has made, biting at her feet and even trying to pull her proboscis away. She puts up with this for a while and then flies off to another tree to start all over again, leaving her aggressors to squabble for drink among themselves until the resins in the sap harden and seal the hole.

Eventually, after she has mated, she will lay eggs in the bark and die, well before autumn sets in. Her adult life has lasted a high summer month or so. You can sometimes see ants devouring her carcase, so that, quite contrary to what La Fontaine has to say, the cicada provides both meat and drink for the ant. The grub born from the egg will drop to the ground, burrow beneath the surface, and will feed on roots for several *years* before surfacing as an unlovely troglodyte out of which the beautiful adult cicada will emerge to dry her flashing wings in the sun.

* * *

Meanwhile . . . rustle, rustle: there's something there, throwing its tiny weight about in the long grass by the steps that lead up to the vegetable garden. A lizard? A mouse? A cricket? Another cicada, even?

Presently the grass parts and allows me, obviously with nothing better to do than stand and stare at French creepy-crawlies, to identify it. No, it's not a cicada. Slender pale green body, about 7cm long, neatly folded wings, bug eyes. The grass-stalk it favours, swinging itself up with its long legs, isn't strong enough to hold its weight and it crashes down like a mistiming pole-vaulter. It clambers up again, finds a stronger stalk and perches there, its muscular saw-edged forelegs drawn up like an old-time prizefighter, or in an attitude suggestive of prayer. It waits. And watches. And waits.

It's a praying mantis. 'Preying' might be a better spelling, because as soon as anything passes in close range of the swivelling bug eyes, PAF! The forelegs shoot out and grip the luckless passer-by, and its lunch is assured. It caught, and dropped, the blade of grass I waved in front of it as many times as I had patience to wave it. No vegetarian, the praying mantis.

The people round here call it 'Marie-Jeanne', unerringly paying attention to the female, and the older country folk, those that still speak Occitan, call it *Lou Prego-Diou*, The Pray-to-God. The male has a pretty rough time of it. During mating the female will turn her head and start to eat her partner. One love-bite too many and you might think any red-blooded male would leg it double quick in search of a less demanding partner, but no: the male mantis puts up with it, content to know that he's nourishing the eggs he's fertilising. I call this total commitment, as the pig said to the hen when arguing about their relative contributions to the breakfast table. Wasn't it Rudyard Kipling who wrote 'The female of the species is more deadly than the male'?

* * *

I lifted most of the technical information about the cicada and the praying mantis from the works of Jean-Henri Fabre, a 19th-century entomologist who wrote about insects with great accuracy but also with such a poetic zeal, rare in a scientist, that he is sometimes known as the Homer of insects. Maybe with reason; his scientific observation is faultless, but his style is something else:

> *These holy airs and graces,* he writes about the praying mantis, *hide the most atrocious manners, those prayerful arms are a horrible brigand's claws! The praying mantis is the tiger of the peaceful race of insects, an ogre in ambush! Her weapons are her legs, for her thigh is a terrible saw with two parallel blades separated by a kind of gutter into which her lower leg, which also has a saw, slots when it is bent . . .*

I discovered Fabre in a book by Eleanor Doorly, probably a deeply unfashionable children's author nowadays, called *The Insect Man*, which my mother gave me for my 11th birthday. Fabre in his various guises of observer, detective, discoverer and seeker after truth fascinated me, and the descriptions of the land he lived and worked in held me fast: *The Insect Man* sowed the first seeds of a deep and abiding love of the Midi. His birthplace, a tiny house with even tinier windows – which tells you something about the local climate – is in St Léons, a village high up on the granite tableland of the Aveyron east of Rodez. An association called *Les Amis de Jean-Henri Fabre* has made it into a little museum, which I'm sure that Fabre, the most modest of men, would have thought a quite excessive tribute to his work. Born into a poor family in 1823, his early history is one of pulling himself up by his bootstraps, a model of self-help, self-reliance and determination to move himself up in the world of science. He paid for his own studies by selling fruit at local markets and by working as a navvy on the railways, at that time spreading all over France, until he won a scholarship to the teacher training college at Avignon. He taught for some 20 years in Carpentras, in Corsica and in Avignon, studying all the time and eventually finishing up with a doctorate from the University of Paris. His early publications included a complete set of natural and applied science textbooks, which appeared in 52 volumes: royalties enabled him to buy in 1879 a property near Orange where he lived for the rest of his life, researching and publishing piecemeal the 10-volume work for which he is best known, his *Souvenirs Entomologiques*, which I suppose you could translate, not very convincingly, as Insect Memories. The tenth and final volume appeared in 1907, by which time he had become the entomologist equivalent of Charles Darwin or Louis Pasteur. His industry extended beyond his passion for insects: he married twice, left behind 9 children and a sizeable body of Provençal verse.

There's a tiny garden attached to his birthplace at St Léons, with a most unusual statue of Fabre in it. The sculptor carved him, broad brimmed hat and all, observing something on a tree-stump, shading his magnifying glass from the glare of the sun by holding his coat up beside his ear. So much more revealing than a straight bust or formal portrait. If it was proposed to make a statue of you, what would you like to be sculpted as doing?

Not as the female praying mantis at her favourite snack, surely.

Service d'été, they call it, summer timetable. It comes in about May and lasts until *la rentrée* in early September, when summer holidays end and the schools go back. *Service d'été* means you start work, particularly if you're employed in active outdoor work like building, at about 5.30 in the morning, just as dawn is breaking. Halfway through the morning you break for coffee and a bite to eat, maybe some slices of sausage or mountain ham sandwiched in a *baguette* and an orange, and you work on till 12.30 or 1 o'clock, when you finish for the day. The exact hours depend on your contract with your employer, very important in French labour laws, and whether you're subject to the 35 hour week, the maximum anyone is allowed to work in France if their company has more than a handful of employees.

The object is to avoid the summer heat. Even we in our modest way follow the *service d'été,* throwing off the covers as the dawn chorus starts and buckling down to the day's demands before the sun and the flies make energetic movement a torture. The first of the *service d'été* tasks is to open all the doors, shutters and windows to let the early morning cool in, a magically sweet air that wafts through the house like a tingle down the spine. Once the cool is in we do our best to keep it in and the sun out, closing doors and windows and leaving the shutters with the merest sliver of daylight showing through.

We learnt this, as most of life's really vital lessons are learnt, the hard way. We truly believed, during summer holidays in France in the years before we came to live here, that the universal shutters were a quaint survival from days when glass was a luxury, a picturesque encumbrance prettifying the country cottages we used to take for two or three July weeks. And as for windows opening inwards, why, that was yet another case of Gallic perversity, something you tolerated with an amused smile, like shameless queue-jumping or double parking. So in our holiday cottage all the windows and all the doors stayed wide open all day, shutters stayed permanently fastened back, the kids finally stopped girning and bellyaching about the heat at 2 o'clock in the morning and everybody slept in a desperate muck-sweat. And the village shop or the local supermarket did a roaring trade in fly-papers, those revolting strips of glued paper you unwind and hang from the ceiling until they're as black as the inside of a Garibaldi biscuit. For the kids counting dead flies was probably the highlight of the French holiday experience.

Service d'été brings with it another inestimable benefit, something so un-British that the word for it doesn't exist in English and we've had to borrow from the Spanish: SIESTA. Down here in the deep South the practice has been given a French dressing: *faire la sieste*, to make the siesta, explains why so many houses go so quiet after lunch in high summer. *Faire la sieste* is more thorough-going than just taking a quick zizz in an armchair, though. Dedicated siesta buffs get themselves fairly and squarely into bed. (What else goes on is anybody's guess. There was a curious theory advanced in the lifestyle section of one of the English Sunday papers that Frenchwomen stayed so slim as a result of sex in the afternoon. *Tout est possible*, everything is possible, of course, especially conjecture.)

Our attempts to drop off the other afternoon were continually frustrated. Every time the blessed tide of sleep was about to lap over us an infernal buzzing started up by the window, indeed in the window frame itself. We put up with it for a bit, hoping it would go away, but after thirty minutes of sleep deprivation I got up to investigate.

All our windows, which came from a national chain of joinery suppliers called Lapeyre, have two or three pencil-wide holes drilled in the bottom rail of the frame, leading into a channel for drainage and ventilation, and I don't suppose that whoever designed them ever gave a thought to the insects these holes would provide an Ideal Home for. I opened the window and there was . . . but I'd better go back a few months.

We opened a window downstairs earlier in the year to discover, in the base of the frame, some tiny shards of the most delicate, finger-nail-thin pottery and at least a hundred dead spiders. Twenty years earlier the kids would have amused themselves counting them or using them as chips in betting games, and the Great Spider Massacre would have found its way into the loom of childhood legend, but we hoovered the lot up, ex-spiders and shards, unable to explain how they'd got there.

Fast forward to our non-siesta. On opening the bedroom window there was a small wasp, making tiny mud capsules and a lot of noise. No spiders, though. So, this was the culprit. I watched for a moment until it – she, actually – buzzed off to garner more mud from the ditch, or maybe the *service d'été* kicked in. Anyway, the noise stopped, peace reigned and we drifted off.

I looked the wasp up later and discovered an extraordinary sequence. She's called *Trypoxylon figulus*. When she's ready to lay eggs she finds a hollow stem or a rock crevice, if there isn't a Lapeyre window handy. She collects jawfuls of mud which she sculpts into little vases. She also collects small spiders, which she paralyses with her sting. When she has collected enough to fill the vase, she lays an egg in it and seals it with a little mud cap. Weeks later, the grub hatches and finds itself in its own private larder. It nourishes itself on whatever juices are to be found in spiders, and when it's ready it bursts out of its vase, scattering desiccated spider cadavers like so many empty Cow and Gate cartons and starts the cycle over again.

Our *Trypoxylon figulus* wasn't like ordinary black and yellow wasps. She was very French, dark as *chocolat noir* and very slender, not to say *svelte*. What female wouldn't be, with such a high-protein diet? And with making good use of the afternoons, of course.

MÉLI-MÉLO

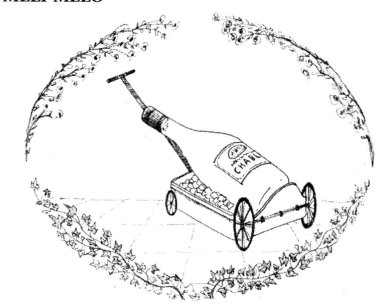

Crossing the Rubicon

I suppose one of the benefits of a classical education is that you know what the Rubicon is. You remember, what you cross when the die is cast, you've burnt your boats, you've made an irrevocable decision and there's no turning back. If you learnt *amo amas amat* at school the chances are you'll know that the Rubicon is an obscure river in northern Italy on which Julius Caesar halted his legions before making the irrevocable decision to march southwards and establish himself as dictator to sort out the political mess Rome had got itself into. Whatever else he may have done he secured a joyful place in the hearts and minds of Latin-learning children everywhere, because when your teacher wasn't looking you could award yourself top marks by translating *Caesar adsum jam forte* as 'Caesar had some jam for tea'.

'What was the worst moment?' people sometimes ask, referring to the decision some fifteen years ago to cross our personal Rubicon, sell up in Scotland and march on the Midi.

I stop to think. Setting up in another country can be pretty daunting, especially one like France, awash with forms that fill the hearts and minds of every *fonctionnaire*. It's not their fault, of course. In an uncertain world forms provide deep comfort and security. It's all the boxes, you see. Those black lines define things, the limits are known. My heart and mind goes out to any fellow EU citizen doing things the other way round, trying to put roots down in Scotland. The sense of individual freedom must be bewildering.

Some of my darkest moments came before the dawn of realising that the Rubicon was a ditch you could step over and not the Pacific Ocean. For instance, we couldn't possibly have left Bellamy the dog and Nibus the cat behind, but there were stern warnings about the consequences of trying to take them into France without this inoculation or that certificate. Several visits to the vet's were put to the test one grey October dawn, driving off the ferry at Le Havre after a night crossing racked with worry about what to do if the animals' papers weren't in order. Was there a customs officer in sight? I could have brought a zoo in unchecked.

Worse was the visa. In 1991 the advice was to go to the French consulate in Edinburgh for a *visa de longue durée*, permission to stay in the country for longer than the 90 days we were allowed as visitors. We understood some French *départements*, administrative areas, were known not to require this. But which? Did they include the Hérault, where we were bound? They weren't listed anywhere. Apparently it depended on the local level of clandestine immigration. Try the *préfecture* of the *département* you're going to, the kind lady at the Edinburgh consulate said: why fork out good money for a visa you don't need? Repeated letters and calls to the relevant desk in Montpellier brought no answer. Time ran out. More sleepless nights. Without the visa, it was said, you couldn't obtain your *carte de séjour*, your residence permit. Without a *carte de séjour* you couldn't work, buy a TV licence or a car, register with the local health authority, or do anything much except breathe and watch furtively for the *gendarmes* coming to escort you back to Le Havre.

I needn't have worried. The *carte de séjour* arrived on production of a bank statement showing that the coffers were full enough to keep the wolf from the door. No whisper of a visa, of course. The good news is that all that has changed, and changed for the better, thanks to Maastricht and similar European Union treaties.

The only procedure still with its Byzantine complications intact, a throwback to unenlightened pre-Maastricht days, a museum piece of bureaucratic obfuscation, is registration with the French health service, which I'm sure has caused many Brits stress-related and psychiatric problems in the same measure as it has denied them the means of treating them. If ever there were tales of woe from expats, they come from dealings with the local health authority. The Holy Grail was more easily accessed than the famous *Carte Vitale*, the green card which is your passport to the French national health service. Baldness among expat men can be entirely attributed to tearing the hair out in exasperation at the *escargot*-like slowness of the process.

You discover, probably by accident, or maybe from the helpful secretary at your local *mairie*, that the issue of green cards is controlled by the CPAM. Having deciphered this acronym, so beloved of the French, as short for *Caisse Primaire d'Assurance Maladie*, primary health insurance pay-desk, you locate the nearest office: it's an hour's journey away. You arrive to find it's market day and parking is a living metaphor for Darwin's ideas of natural selection and survival of the fittest. You get lost in the maze of narrow town-centre streets, you end up parking half on the pavement, half in a bus lane, you finally arrive at the CPAM at 11.40. A receptionist tells you to take a numbered ticket from a dispenser. It says 467. It's a sequence ticket, you'll be seen after whoever holds number 466. At present number 463 is being seen in the one open interview booth, a large African family. At 11.55 the

Africans decamp, the interviewer shuts up shop. No explanation. A fellow-waiter tells you in a sort of pidgin-Franglais to come back in the afternoon. You kick your heels for a couple of hours, your temper sorely tried by a) a parking ticket which doesn't tell you how to deal with it, and b) your partner, who keeps reminding you that he/she did urge you not to park there, but you're so bloody pigheaded etc., etc.

A deeply suspicious interviewer eventually sees you at 14.50. She screws up her eyes trying to understand the sentences you've carefully rehearsed. She interrupts you to give you a list of the documents you'll need to support your application. She tells you come back when you've collected them all.

We fast forward through weeks of paperchasing to the day when the dossier is finally complete. You choose a non-market day for your second visit to the CPAM, starting much earlier in the morning. You're learning fast. Miracles of miracles, there's a parking slot right outside the building. A very charming young man receives you. He knows England, he says, in fact his sister lives in Baxton. You feel slightly ashamed that you don't know where this place is. He congratulates you in excellent English on the quality, presentation and comprehensive nature of your dossier. Everything is in order and your green cards will be despatched to you very soon. You thank him with tears in your eyes. You treat yourselves to a celebratory lunch.

Eight weeks pass and nothing happens. By this time the validity of some of your supporting documents has expired. Lacking confidence on the telephone, you visit the CPAM again. A smiling, efficient woman tells you she is *désolée*, desolated, but nobody has heard of you. There's no trace of any application or dossier in your name. All she can do is give you another application form and list of required documents. She is genuinely sorry: the best she can offer is temporary emergency cover if you're destitute and homeless. You consider for a moment whether this mightn't be the best course, to start camping out with your begging bowl on the steps of the CPAM, but in the event you go outside and burst into tears.

In due course the wretched thing arrives, but by that time you've probably returned to the UK, been sectioned or have croaked.

* * *

At one time my *carte de séjour* (they've since been abolished) came up for renewal. No bank statements this time, but a new form to complete. French forms have a style all of their own. The *carte de séjour* application form was a shining example, aglow with a hidden agenda. Adepts at interpreting official form reference numbers could probably have dated it circa 1956:

> Did you enter the country clandestinely?
> Have you rendered notable service to France?
> Have any fines been paid off?
> Have any of your ascendants or descendants served under
> French colours?
> Are you claiming political asylum?
> Have you been awarded any French decorations?

Hand on heart I answered *non, non, oui* (I was once done for speeding), *non, non, non* and hoped for the best. The final, decisive section of the form was reserved for the *maire's* recommendation. I hoped my service as the Olargues Titular Organist would count favourably: at any rate my *carte de séjour* was renewed effortlessly. But then, as you've maybe noticed already, we expats have got the local vote now.

Near Olargues there are hamlets called Cailho (pronounced kye-o) and Julio, ample proof, if you listen to some of the locals, that Caius Julius Caesar holed up here once. However, Caesar's baldness is well documented. It seems clear to me that if he needed to put time by in Olargues, he was waiting for his *Carte Vitale* and tearing his hair out the while. If we'd been around at the time, we'd have been glad to take him in. We could even have made sure that he *adsum jam forte.*

Le Golden Oldie

Is Desert Island Discs still on the go? You know, the radio programme where the guests are invited to list the music they'd take with them if they were in for a long stay on a desert island? Years ago I used to listen to it occasionally when it was hosted by a gentlemanly chap called Roy Plomley, and then I have an idea Sue Lawley took it over, and after that it's just one more of those things that have fallen into a post-moving-to-France limbo.

The question came to me the other day when a kind friend, gratifyingly aware of my weaknesses, returned from a quick sortie to the UK with a copy of *Private Eye* in one hand and a couple of green and gold tins in the other. These tins featured, as they've done for donkey's years, a dead lion with bees buzzing around the carcase.

You'll have recognised the product, I expect: Golden Syrup. The technical name for this nectar is partially inverted refiner's syrup, apparently. What a dead lion's doing on the tin is no mystery to those who can find their way to the Old Testament, Judges Chapter 14, where it features in the story of Samson, a man who would have had some fairly unusual experiences to relate on Desert Island Discs.

UK supermarket shelves may buckle under the weight of Golden Syrup, but here in the Midi you're more likely to come across a dead lion lying by the roadside than the famous Biblical tin on the shelves of supermarket giants Auchan or E.Leclerc. Somehow the French have survived and more or less held together as a nation without the help of Golden Syrup, or Marmite, digestive biscuits, HP Sauce or Lucozade. One is what one eats, of course. I'm afraid I can't think of any British achievements soundly based on croissants, *foie gras* or haricot beans. There's obviously no substitute for Mother's Pride, Baked Beans and Branston Pickle, all as vital to the process of national body-building as canned spinach is to Popeye the Sailorman.

If you were cast away on a desert island, which foods would you take with you? In the original radio programme you were allowed the Bible, in case you needed to brush up on Judges Chapter 14, and Shakespeare as your staple reading material, but there was never any mention of staple diet. Golden Syrup? Pot Noodles? Sticky Toffee Pudding? Many expats down here must have asked themselves the same question, fearful that surrender to the sun also meant surrender to the French diet. Not much wrong with that, in my opinion, in fact quite the reverse, but clearly not everyone thinks as I do: in our time we've come across an expat couple from Goole called Ron and Julie, known in accordance with our genetic inability to leave a perfectly good name alone as The Ghoulies. Their spare room wardrobe is stacked from floor to ceiling with tins of Bird's Custard Powder and Heinz Beans against the day when the balloon goes up, there's a general uprising against expats and a siege has to be withstood until the SAS breaks through and helicopters them back to Blighty and more Birds and baked beans.

Anyway, some irrational school dinner nostalgia must have seized me recently, because for an anniversary treat I'd set my heart on treacle tart, again not a thing that's readily available in France. Diet-wise, for one whose arteries tend to clog up at the very whisper of refined carbohydrates, treacle tart should be labelled with the health warning you get here with every mention of alcohol: *L'abus est dangéreux pour la santé. A consommer avec modération.* Misuse is a health risk. Don't over-indulge. But just once couldn't do much harm, surely?

In due course a gorgeous smiling treacle tart appeared on the dinner table, glowing with partially inverted refiner's syrup like the setting sun on a golden summer evening, in the presence not only of ourselves but of the donor as well; an offering, a celebration of Britishness, a lest-we-forget token of our heritage, our roots, our origins in This blessed plot, this earth, this realm, this England, This nurse, this teeming womb of royal kings and all the rest of it.

Well, we didn't enjoy it at all. We'd just lost the taste for it, it seemed. It was no use saying why, it needs custard (which the French, incidentally, call *crème anglaise*, English cream, and serve cold, thin and over-sweet), let's just nip down to The Ghoulies and make them give us a tin of Bird's, the anti-expat pogroms aren't going to start tonight. It was a sad, sad disappointment. And I'd looked forward to it so much. Sometimes it's better to travel in hope than to arrive, of course. The situation begged a few questions: are we going native? Have we lived in France too long? Have we lost our need for comfort foods like treacle tart? Oh dear, what's happened to us?

Then . . . going into a supermarket in Pézenas a few days ago, just at the start of the holiday season, what should there be but a tum-warming display of British goodies, everything I've mentioned so far and more, far more: Bisto gravy granules, tinned chocolate sponge, piccalilli, mushroom soup. I was just deploring holidaymakers going for this sort of thing instead of surrendering joyfully to the heady seductions of local restaurants, when something loomed up off the shelves that scotched these toffee-nosed notions: a noble pile, indeed a holy mountain of Ambrosia Creamed Rice. Instant seduction. Wow. That night I ate a whole tin – not out of the tin, there are certain limits – and any fears of batrachomorphosis vanished instantly.

Word travelled round, and various other expat blokes, gentlemanly chaps all, really got quite excited on hearing about this benison at Pézenas. Clearly British dietary genes, however deeply devoted to French cuisine, need the occasional reassuring shot of nursery-thick, hot, rich, creamy rice pudding. The upshot of this is the foundation of a new club meeting on Wednesday nights, when our womenfolk are generally out doing other things: the ACRONYM club. What does it stand for? I'll leave you to guess the ACR bit, and as for the rest, *Oui, Nous (nous) Y Mettons*, yes, we pitch into it.

And batrachomorphosis? H'm, not an easy word. I doubt if you'll find it in the dictionary. The Greek 'batrachos' (frog) and 'morphosis' (change into another state) may give a clue. I'm glad to be able to tell you I'm not suffering from it. I'll tell you more if I ever appear on Desert Island Discs. Correction: that should read Dessert Island Discs, with my tin of ACR, naturally.

You've got two minutes. Two minutes to write down all the French words you can think of that we use in ordinary everyday English speech. Nonsense, there are hundreds of them. You've got pencil, paper and watch? Right, head down and off you go.

Baton, reservoir, magazine. Blancmange, garage, bureau. Splendid! *Programme, crayon, masseur. Plaque, casserole, contretemps.* Here, this is really good. *Fiancé, dessert, questionnaire. Hotel, sabotage, cigarette.* Wonderful! Now just keep going while I develop my theme . . .

You see my point? We're not exactly innocent of word-theft across the Channel. For every linguistic booze-cruise descending on the Channel ports, there's a steady flow of dictionary plunder in the other direction. Certainly from south of the Channel, from here in the Deep South, you might think the traffic was all one way, and that the thieving French regularly plundered our dictionaries and made off with the loot in sacks marked *le swag*. And some loot!

Our British eyebrows reach for the ceiling when we come across in *Midi Libre*, our local newspaper, the expression *le starting-block* in an article about athletics, or *le melting-pot* in a report about EU fishing policy, or *le gentleman-farmer* in a piece about style. Stolen and indeed laundered linguistic goods feature strongly in the endless handouts we find in our letter-box. Here's one from Intermarché, a national chain of supermarkets, the size of a broadsheet newspaper featuring enormous mouth-watering cuts of succulent beef. The meat's produced, the blurb says, in the European Union, but there's an asterisk directing you to a tiny footnote: *hormis Royaume Uni*, United Kingdom excepted. Aha. They won't take our meat, but they'll take our word for it: *le steack* at so much per kilo.

You could be forgiven, looking through these handouts, for wondering why you bothered to learn all that French vocab. back in

5th year. It's strange that in the land of *haute couture* articles of everyday clothing in France should have reach-me-down names from across the Channel and from beyond the Atlantic: if you spoke not a word of French you could still kit yourself out quite comprehensively night and day in local clothing stores with *le jean, le T-shirt, le short, le pyjama, le sweat* (i.e. sweatshirt), *le pullover* for when there's a nip in the air, *les baskets* (trainers, what you play basketball in) and *les tennis* for informal footwear, not to mention *le smoking* (i.e. dinner jacket) for more formal occasions. As for *le slip* . . . in crossing the Channel *le slip* has undergone an interesting change: here it refers to a style of male underpants, which come in various sizes, *patron, grand patron, super patron, pacha* (i.e. pasha), etc.

All these are pronounced as though they were French (and who's to blame them?) and we flounder helplessly sometimes, quite unable to recognise our own. Christian the builder from Félines Minervois, whom we've met once or twice before, occasionally recommended something called 'wees pirree' for this or that task. We surrendered, totally lost. What could he mean? Eventually we fell in behind him as he marched to the boiler room, where we kept general household and DIY products. He pointed to a bottle labelled 'White Spirit'.

Sometimes it's more abstruse. In the days when I lived in the Tarn *département* I once asked M. Renard, the amiable proprietor of l'Oustalet, the café-restaurant (you see, it really does work both ways) in the village of Lacabarède, how he was. Not bad, he supposed, but his view of the world would have been less jaundiced if his 'babbeefoot' hadn't been broken. 'Babbeefoot' was a new one on me: a bone in the foot, maybe? So much of understanding French, in the early stages of a conversation before your ear is fully tuned, depends on identifying the keyword and reacting appropriately, even though much of what surrounds the keyword goes over your head. I didn't know how to react. Perhaps I should have said 'How painful for you! Have you been to the doctor?' but I wasn't certain so I just nodded non-committally. I expect I got a black mark in the kitchens and an extra dose of pepper in the *sauce diable* to spice up this hard and heartless *Anglais*, typically unsympathetic to M. Renard's desperate plight.

It turned out that 'babbeefoot' was Babyfoot, the manic miniature football game that he keeps in his bar, the one where you twiddle the knobs furiously and your row of full backs spin in unison somersaults and propel the ball violently into your own goal. A shame for M. Renard, but I can't say I felt all that deprived, having gone for *un steack* and not for *un match de foot*.

But those keywords . . . sometimes, however long you wait, they just never come, and you discover that you've let your interlocutor gabble on far too long to say 'I'm sorry, I haven't understood a single word. Would you begin again, please? Slowly?' Instead you smile weakly, say Ah! with selected grimaces which might be taken to express agreement or disagreement, whichever suits the case. You suffer worse agonies than a pain in the babbeefoot. Sometimes you pick up the keyword without being any the wiser. I remember a conversation with the Kalashnikov-voiced Jean Arcas, *maire* of Olargues. The keywords that emerged from what he was trying to tell me was *à la poule*.

A la poule gave nothing away. To the hen? In the style of the hen? I knew that colloquially *poule* can mean dolly-bird, chick, bit of skirt etc., but this didn't quite fit the bill. It seemed to be something he'd had experience of, something he'd enjoyed, something I must know about too. I became aware of a strong Scottish connection. It seemed he'd actually been to Scotland. Recently. Some escapade with a Scottish floozie? Surely not.

A la poule, à la poule, à la poule. No, not a hope. The only connection I could make between poultry and Scotland was cock-a-leekie soup. H'm. Not a man to detain one long in conversation, M. Arcas made off before I could volunteer to produce a recipe, but in parting he invited us to a reception at the *mairie* the following Sunday morning.

The tricolor was flying from the *mairie* balcony, something that only happens on special occasions. In the reception room the *conseil municipal*, the village council, had gathered round the bar at one end, while at the other, beneath the official portrait of the President, was something like a Harvest Festival altar, a table laden with local produce, the splendid honey, cheeses, smoked and cured meats, pâtés, chestnut products, olive oil and wine that it has been such a joy to get to know. No hens, however. Someone had gone to a lot of trouble. Carefully composed bouquets of herbs – thyme, rosemary, savory – that so richly scent the *garrigue*, the Mediterranean upland scrub, lay awaiting presentation. But the centrepiece was an arrangement of three flags, the tricolor of France, the twelve stars of the European Union and the dark blue and white St Andrew's cross (aye, I ken fine, a diagonal cross is really a saltire) of Scotland.

The guests of honour were a most unexpected quartet from the north of Scotland, representatives from the Highland Council, the Highland Enterprise Board and the local education authority in the person of the Rector of Ullapool High School, a noted geologist. In fact the whole affair marked the start of the return leg of a Brussels-financed geological exchange visit, from the geologically rich hinterland of the Hérault *département* to the equally varied rocks and strata of Wester Ross and vice versa. Speeches were made in very competent French by Isobel from Inverness and in equally competent English, a rarity here, by Pierre Teillaud, director of the Olargues environmental centre. M. Arcas spoke enthusiastically of the jolly time he'd had in *à la poule*, gifts were exchanged, the bar declared open. I don't know why we were there, except as longstop interpreters if necessary.

However our services weren't required, and just as well after the *à la poule* fiasco. You've seen it, of course? M. Arcas meant *Ullapool*. I can only say I'm glad he didn't climb Cul Mor, a mountain in Wester Ross, geological hammer in hand: this would have come out as *cul mort*, meaning dead bum – and even that's a euphemism – which just about sums up my wild guesswork. Cock-a-leekie soup, my babbeefoot.

A few governments ago the Keep French Pure lobby prevailed upon a M. Toubon, then Minister of Culture, to act decisively against the growing adulteration of French with imports like *le babyfoot* and *le british look*, not to mention virtually the entire IT vocabulary. Most of these Anglo-Saxon additives come from across the Atlantic rather than across the Channel, in what Paris journalists have coined *la coca-colonisation*. They're probably the same journalists who called M. Toubon, very unfeelingly, Mr Allgood.

Mr Allgood should have left well alone, even though for a while we heard less of *le weekend* on radio and television and more of *la fin de semaine*, less of *le leader* and more of *le chef*, less *le mél* (i.e. e-mail) and more of *le courriel*. Not for long, though: language grows at its own pace, and you can't do much to stunt its growth. Why, the other day we shared a lift in Montpellier with a young Frenchman who said *OK, je speed* into his mobile. No translation needed. Imagine The National Trust or indeed The Saltire Society urging the minister for the arts and culture to ban . . . well, how are you getting on with that list?

. . . *fête, morale, bonhomie. Entente cordiale,*
joie de vivre, camaraderie . . .

that's more like it. Touch them at your peril – English has such need of them!

Memory department

A few summers ago some fairly elderly friends came to swim, and a little poolside chat revealed that Moïse, 68 and counting, was increasingly afflicted with senior moments. He had an awful problem, he said, with the simplest things, his children's names, why he'd gone into his garage, where the salt was kept. The answers came to him eventually, after enormous effort. He put this weakness down to mental disorganisation, so he said he was going to train his mind with regular exercise and iron discipline.

First, he was going to learn by heart the numbers of the French *départements*. The *départements* are the administrative divisions of France, like counties in the UK or the USA. They date from the Napoleonic aftermath of the French Revolution, when the old provinces (Touraine, Béarn, Languedoc, Berri and so on) were abandoned in favour of smaller, more easily administered units, in which the golden rule was that it had to be possible to ride on horseback from the centre to any point in one day.

Mostly the new units were named after geographical features, like the Dordogne from the river that flows through it, or like the Jura from the mountains that cover much of it. But not all: one, indeed, the Calvados in Normandy, seems to be named after a fiery distillation from apples, but I expect there's another reason. Much later they were given numbers, and the most obvious manifestation of this today is on vehicle number plates, where the last two figures refer to the *département* the car is registered in. More recently they've been used as the basis of post-codes, where the first two numbers of the five-figure post-code denote the *département*, and if ever you want your mail to be delayed you have only to miss it out on the envelope.

So this is what Moïse set himself to do, to learn all the *département* numbers, from 01 (Ain) to 95 (Val d'Oise), a task slightly eased by their being roughly in alphabetical order. But that wasn't all for Moïse. Learning what the French call *les numéros mineralogiques* wasn't anything like stringent enough: next on the agenda were the French area telephone codes. *Un défi*, a challenge, to be sure, but he was determined to show his memory who was boss.

* * *

Maybe something Moïse could have tried is an in-car game designed to reduce levels of boredom in the back during long journeys in France.

The rules are simple. Allow yourself any French vehicle in any situation, moving, parked, clamped, in a used car lot, scrap heap, anywhere except in a picture or on a television screen. (You may be tempted to these expedients as the game becomes desperate or even suicidal.) The trigger, the starting point is seeing a vehicle with 01 as the last two numbers on its registration plate, meaning that it comes from the Ain *département*, north-east of Lyon and bordering Switzerland. You're off: nothing will content you until you've seen 02, then 03, 04 (Alpes de Haute Provence), 05 (Hautes Alpes) and 06 (Alpes Maritimes, so the vehicle probably comes from Nice). By this time you're hooked, a regular obsessive calling down curses on the heads of the palsied inhabitants of the Ardèche (07) who never allow you so much as a distant glimpse of their wretched wheels, and threatening with blue murder not only the entire population of the Ardennes (08) for lying so invisibly low but also the driver of the car who says casually *09? Ariège? Why, I saw one only 10 minutes ago when we stopped for petrol. Don't tell me you missed it!* Because, of course, you have to see it with your own eyes: no proxies allowed. And if your passengers start suing each other for criminal assault, malfeasance and perjury don't come grumbling to me about it. I only mentioned relief of boredom.

Months later I asked Moïse how he was getting on. Not well, he said: he'd maybe over-reached himself after all. 01 – Ain; 02 – Aisne; 03 – Allier, he told me, but he stuck at 04. He knew them, but he just couldn't call them to mind. A film of sadness passed over his eyes: he would have hoped that someone called Moïse (the French for Moses) would have been able to get up to 10 at least.

A is for August

A for August, the soldier month, the Anglo-French poet Hilaire Belloc calls it, I don't quite know why; most people are only too glad to lay down their arms – and legs and head and all the rest, and just flop out *flagada tout mou*, if you want a nice little drop of friendly colloquial French to see you through your poolside siesta. Or, if you're female, *flagada toute molle*. So gender-polite, the French, although an American friend berates their insensitivity in insisting on the masculinity of making something so essentially maternal as milk: *le lait*.

However philology isn't the first activity that springs to mind after one of those wonderful alfresco poolside lunches of *baguette*, cheese, sausage and olives, sun-warmed tomatoes and peaches, and of course an extra nice little drop of friendly colloquial *rosé* to round off the corners; but just when you thought it was safe to stretch out on your lounger and surrender, suddenly . . .

. . . why do children, small, big and especially adult, feel obliged to make such an infernal racket round the pool, when all you want is to hear beyond your siesta dreams is the gentle, somnolent lap-lapping of still waters? Never mind children; staid besuited businessmen, grim head teachers, even beaming ministers of religion go absolutely ape when they get anywhere near a swimming pool. What primeval, Darwinian urges get amongst them?

Once we entertained round our pool the Goldberg Ensemble, a Viennese string quartet. Siesta? Dream on. It was a wonder any water was left in the pool after they'd finished leaping in, splashing and sloshing, jumping on each other, playing at horsey-back fights, urging each other with frenetic Viennese imprecations to wilder and wilder abandon. Blood flowed from the 'cellist's nose at one point, in the manic rush of their water-play. And these are dedicated musicians who normally spend their time pouring out the deepest utterances of Beethoven and Brahms. Maybe that's why.

* * *

A for . . . well, 'Orses, to quote a sort of Cockney alphabet that intrigued me as a child (B for mutton, C for miles, it went on: you could continue it if you've honestly got nothing better to do), and horses featured strongly at an August country wedding we went to where the bride and groom got themselves hitched in the saddle.

Well, more or less. The indispensable civil ceremony, performed by the lady *maire* of St Nom le Château, was followed by the optional church ceremony in the neighbouring village of St Nom le Vieux, a mere kilometre away by winding lane and farm track. Bride and groom chose to ride to the church and back, so outside the *mairie* Didier, shortly to enter La Garde Republicaine, an ultra-smart cavalry formation something like the Household Brigade in the UK but composed of policemen, mounted Elan, while Magali, his bride of a few minutes, in full off-white wedding dress, arranged herself side-saddle on Kiki. So they trotted off into matrimony, prettiest of pictures in the summer sun, followed by a procession of about 50 cars with strict orders to defy French wedding tradition by not sounding their horns continually for fear of upsetting the horses.

Side-saddle? The French have a word for it, of course: *A l'amazone.* A for Amazon, absolutely.

* * *

A for aftermath . . . the French certainly have the knack of ensuring that at wedding banquets no one peaks too early, slides discreetly under the table and spends the rest of the night there, blotto: as soon as the hors d'oeuvres buffet, lubricated from a bottle of Chablis so immense (a Psalmannazar, in fact) that it had to be wheeled about in a little cart, had been cleared away, the disco started. Whirling, sharp-edged French accordion waltzes and good old classic stompers like *Brown Girl in the Ring* and *Rah Rah Rasputin* settle the stomach amazingly well, and when at last we tired of waving our arms about for *YMCA*, inevitably followed by *In The Navy*, they served the main course.

Then more dancing, followed an hour and more later by the next course, and so it went on until they finally served onion soup by the dawn light. Or so we were told at the survivors' lunch the next day, because we'd run out of puff long before then. No indigestion or sense of the slightest hangover, though, thanks to all that between-course dancing. In fact I think YMCA probably stands for Your Main Course Awaits. No? Well, you think of something better.

* * *

A for *aoûtas*. August (*août* in French, economically pronounced 'oot') gives its name to the annual crop of *aoûtas*, the vicious little no-see-'em brutes, minute midges that attack unseen all those inaccessible places that leave you itching to have a really good scratch. Which just makes it worse, of course.

A minor summer mystery is how they get behind your knees when you're wearing trousers or how they've managed to ravage your ankles at night when you're tucked up securely. Never mind. Do your worst, *aoûtas*: we've discovered a miracle cure, a clear ointment called Butix, available from your local *pharmacie*. There's even a repellent called Pre-Butix, just the thing to slap on with the suntan oil for a peaceful siesta by the pool, undisturbed by no-see-'ems, string quartets, brown girls in rings, Rasputin, etc. Sweet dreams.

Striking the Changing Hour

The clocks went back last weekend. I used to have a small problem remembering which way they went until an American taught me a simple mnemonic: Spring Forward, Fall Back. Very useful if you speak English, but not much cop in France, I'm afraid. It won't translate into a snappy little expression to help horally-challenged French or their expat guests to remember they've got an extra hour to lie in bed pondering that 'spring' has at least four meanings: *ressort*, as in mattress; *printemps*, the season; *sauter*, meaning to jump; and *source*, meaning where the best water to dilute your *pastis* comes from.

So the clocks went back and clearly it didn't suit everyone. It became a scapegoat – *un bouc émissaire*, if you want a snappy little idiom to stun your French evening class with – a scapegoat for France's ills, big and small.

As we adjust slowly to the change of hour we find ourselves actually waiting for the TV news instead of being late for it and sometimes missing it altogether. On *La Une*, as TF1 is popularly known, which equates more or less with BBC1, you can tell how desperate the news is going to be by the choice of news reader. If it's not too bad, France has squeezed a draw at football away to Greenland, the CAC40, the Paris *bourse* share index, has only dropped seven points, some Corsican separatists only just managed to escape, they put a news reader with the splendid name of Patrick Poivre d'Armor in to bat.

If the news is good, France beat Greenland 1-0 in the return match, CAC40 stocks have risen, the Corsican separatists have been arrested and turned out to be policemen anyway, a classically attractive news reader called Claire Chazal (whom the gossip columns have been known to link romantically with PPd'A) shares the general euphoria. But if the news is uniformly awful, they put in Jean-Pierre Pernaut, because he makes everything seem so much more cheerful. We've been seeing a lot of Jean-Pierre Pernaut recently. He does the strikes, for one thing, and he manages to put such a gloss of stoical cheerfulness on them, and indeed on anything that mankind could really do without, that you're obliged to think that maybe the French nation isn't grinding to a halt just yet.

As far as I know nobody has ever gone on strike over putting the clocks back, but it may be early days. There were some farmers complaining recently that the new milking timetable had upset their cows. Well, if France's dairy farmers want to make their point by going on strike, presumably on behalf of their cows, there's a limited slot available for them, because just now the schools are on holiday for the traditional autumn fortnight known as *Toussaint*, All Saints.

Before *Toussaint* kicked in every news bulletin was framed round *les lycéens*, the French senior secondary school pupils. Thousands and thousands of *lycéens* took to the streets of every major French city, chanting, waving banners, demanding more teachers, better conditions, smaller classes and less time-wasting, a set of requirements boiling down to more work and longer hours, not a common demand among strikers. The organisation and coordination of the *lycéens'* strike was thorough and efficient, a tribute as much to their determination as to the facilities the internet and mobile present for this sort of thing. The *lycéens* are cast in a national tradition of protest, of course, and few can have passed through school without having enjoyed regular days off because their teachers were on strike. Even in lowly, remote Olargues teachers have been known to down chalk and picket the school gate.

Industrial unrest in schools doesn't impinge on me as much now as it did in the days when I was a head teacher in Scotland. Indeed, it was really quite uplifting to think well, it's not my problem any more when, driving up the village street once to get my hair trimmed by the amiable M. Soriano I came across a road block outside the primary school, manned by arm-banded pickets. Clearly the teachers were at the end of their tether, although it seemed to me that their cheerful fag-in-mouth holiday air wasn't quite at one with the seething discontent and sense of outrage expressed on their placards and banners. They waved me through with no attempt to put their case and presently I was installed a bit further up the street in M. Soriano's barbershop.

M. Soriano used to think I was Belgian, I suppose on the strength of reasonable French spoken with a strong northern accent. *Much rain up there in Belgium, is there?* he would occasionally ask in his barberly way, or *bad year for aubergines, they say: you Belgians grow many aubergines up your way?* It took some time to convince him that I was no more Belgian than he was Claire Chazal, but this just had the effect of replacing one set of national stereotypes with another. In the matter of industrial relations, M. Soriano revealed, the UK is viewed as a green and pleasant, if rain-soaked, land where no strikes spoil the perfect co-existence between management and workforce.

M. Soriano isn't alone in attributing this supposed harmony to *la dame de fer*, the Iron Lady, Madame Thatcher. She wouldn't have wasted any time, he said, sorting out that nonsense down the road outside the primary school, didn't I agree? I passed on this, partly because Lady T's achievements will remain controversial for many more years than I have hairs left for M. Soriano to snip at disconsolately, and partly because I wasn't sure what they were striking about. What was more, neither did M. Soriano.

At midday, when everything here stops for lunch, even village road blocks, I re-passed the school to read the banners more closely. It was a *cri de cœur* familiar to anyone who had taught in rural Scotland: Olargues felt remote from the regional capital, Montpellier. Their cries for another teacher had gone unheeded. Classes of 38 children of mixed ages imposed impossible working conditions. They'd made every conceivable representation. There was nothing left but to strike.

A day or two later I spoke about it casually to the *maire*, at one the frequent official receptions I get asked to on the doubtful grounds, it seems to me, of being Titular Organist. The *maire* is head of the local *collège* and sits on a large number of local government committees.

Ah, the strike, he said, well, maybe we'd better not say too much about that. *J'ai agressé M. l'Inspecteur de l'Académie. Agresser* means to attack, either verbally or physically . . . it's unthinkable, of course, especially as *M. l'Inspecteur* is a cross between Director of Education and HM Inspector of Schools. No ordinary punchbag. If the *maire* really had clipped him round the ear I'm not certain which TV news reader they would have trotted out to announce it.

* * *

The French expression for a reasonably peaceful demonstration, where few get knocked about, not much property is put to the sack and where the riot police aren't called out, is *atmosphère bon enfant*, meaning that the participants have conducted themselves like well-behaved children. This was as superfluous as it was true of the *lycéens'* strike at Toussaint. A few teachers tried to muscle in, to show an uneasy solidarity with their pupils, but this wasn't universally welcome. 'Our *manifestations'* (a much better word than the mealy-mouthed 'industrial action') say the bright, articulate and very determined young people interviewed by TF1, 'have nothing to do with the unions nor with politics.We're above all that. We are France's future. Mistreat us at your peril.'

On the Wednesday before *Toussaint* – Wednesday isn't a school day in France – *les retraités*, the pensioners, took over the slot vacated by *les lycéens*, and thousands of them parsalysed central Marseilles for hours, Jean-Pierre Pernaut reported. 'This isn't about politics,' their leaders say when interviewed. 'We're above all that. We are France's past. Mistreat us and it will be May '68 all over again.' May '68 refers to the stirring – or shameful, depending on how you line up with M. Soriano – semi-revolution when student protests, stiffened by the trade unions, brought down General de Gaulle. A certain Danny Cohn-Bendit made a name for himself as a revolutionary student leader: he's now a respectable MEP, although a bit on the unkempt side. He could probably do with a visit to M. Soriano.

Thomas Enjalbert down the road is a bit young to remember all that. So is his mother. He's just three, and a handful. He was having his own *manifestation* when I walked past the Enjalberts' the other day on my way to M. Gosset for bread. There certainly wasn't *une atmosphère bon enfant.* His mother Liliane was roaring at him for refusing to get out of the car and – who knows? – maybe my presence saved him from being hauled out bodily by Liliane's beefy forearm and *une fessée,* a hefty smack on the bottom, but I bet he got it hot and strong afterwards.

I sympathised. *C'est pas évident, des fois.* It's not always easy. Liliane agreed. It was changing the hour that upset everyone, including Thomas. He was *infernal.* Worse than all those strikers, any day. A clear case for Jean-Pierre Pernaut.

PEOPLE

Quality control

There doesn't seem to have been any lessening of the popularity of beauty contests in France. Maybe this isn't surprising in a country capable of running *The Benny Hill Show* as emergency fodder whenever French TV studio technicians go on strike, so it's entirely possible that millions of French people base their typical image of the UK on Benny Hill, master of nudge-nudge wink-wink innuendo. The annual Miss France contest is presided over by a patrician chaperone of extreme elegance and rectitude, Madame Geneviève de Fontenay, who wears so large a hat throughout the proceedings that the camera plotting probably has to be scheduled round it. It's unlikely that Geneviève de Fontenay has ever watched *The Benny Hill Show*.

There are preliminary regional heats, and the winners going through to the national final wear sashes saying Miss Provence, Miss

Midi-Pyrénées, Miss Brittany, Miss Alsace and so on. Overseas France isn't forgotten, either: final line-up sashes may also read Miss Martinique or Miss Nouvelle Calédonie. All this to tell you the extraordinary news that only yesterday, carried away by a twinge of the old trouble, viz. Benny Hillitis, I spent a few agreeable moments in the arms and capacious bosom of Marie-Ange, a more than worthy Miss Normandie. Every dog has his day.

(Did I hear you murmur Miss Normandie WHEN? All right, all right. Truth will out. Miss Normandie 1958, if you really want to know. Why must you always prick the bubble of these little fantasies?)

Her husband Albert was there, a man much given to composing flowery (everlasting flowers in some cases, I'm afraid) speeches, odes in prose, to grace whatever occasion he might have been invited to. In this case we'd all foregathered at a *vin d'honneur* in the village of Les Issarts to celebrate some friends' golden wedding: Lazare – whom we've met before at the Olargues *fête du marron* – and his wife Pauline, who sings soprano in Le Choeur des Hauts Cantons. In the village church the bride of 50 years ago had sung, solo, unaccompanied and not without a tear or two, the *Benedictus* from a Schubert mass we'd learnt. After the service the family and guests assembled in the shade of a spreading chestnut tree where white-napered tables groaned under the weight – fast reducing, it has to be said – of bottles of *pastis* and *muscat* and a delectable champagne-based punch called *marquisette*, while there was the usual selection of nibbles: canapés, nuggets of *fougasse* (olive oil based bread with pieces of olive and bacon embedded in it), slices of peppered sausage . . .

After the initial encounter – we hadn't seen Marie-Ange nor Albert for at least four days, and they're extrovert people – she gave us some interesting insights into the world of Miss France. Slices of peppered sausage were not advised, for instance, not simply because they threatened the vital statistics but because bits stuck in your teeth and flavoured your breath with meaty garlic. Not a plus when being interviewed by Madame Geneviève de Fontenay.

Albert had his two-penn'orth to throw in as well, and I suspect there may be quite a story somewhere here. He'd been involved with many Miss France contests, he told me. On the celebratory ode side, I wondered? A sort of poet laureate to the contest? Not really, he said: he'd been more into Quality Control. Fascinated, I pressed for details. It was nothing much, he said modestly: his job had been to make sure the contestants were what they claimed to be.

You mean . . . I began, but at this moment a press photographer whisked him away to take his picture with the Golden Oldies as if in mid-ode, leaving Marie-Ange chatting away with us. Forewarned by the talk of the village, we were careful to avoid a certain subject: like 'don't mention the war' when talking to Germans – although this is fast becoming meaningless, and not before time, as the years roll on – the watchword was 'don't mention the Mediterranean'. What the Mediterranean had done to cause this embargo . . . well, I'll put it in scenario form:

CAST:

Marie-Ange.

Aristide. Sage and philosopher. Rich experience from unusually varied career for a Frenchman. Is capable of starting conversation 'When I was a messenger at the Vatican . . .' or 'When I was training the Peruvian General Staff . . .' or 'In the days when I ran my pedicure salon . . .' Present enthusiasms: The Hundred Years' War, tango, laser surgery, geomorphology.

Jacques. Retired osteopath and willing horse. Always busy with something in the village. Runs the amenity standards watchdog committee, just the man. Level-headed, sane, well-read.

Pascal. Retired hairdresser.

Jean. Retired *vigneron.*

Enric. Retired policeman

Pierre-Marie. Retired lorry driver.

Scene 1: The village pavement, outside M. Rebizoulet's *épicerie*, where there's a railing everyone can lean on. Aristide is giving an unsolicited lecture to Pascal, Jean, Enric and Pierre-Marie, a sort of Greek chorus, about the movements of the earth's tectonic plates. The African plate is moving north, trying to insert itself underneath the European plate. Like an elephant trying to get underneath the bedclothes, he says. The upheaval means the Mediterranean will disappear and all the water will pour back out into the Atlantic through the Straits of Gibraltar. At this point Marie-Ange, split-skirted and all ears, emerges from M. Rebizoulet's. The Greek chorus forsakes consideration of infinitesimally slow geomorphological movements, paced over millions of years, for the immediacy of a glimpse of fleshy white thigh, the same thighs that probably gave them the hots on black and white TV back in the late 50s.

Scene 2: The village museum, staffed by local volunteers. On duty: Jacques and Marie-Ange. Jacques is labelling some local archaeological finds. To his surprise he hears Marie-Ange telling some visitors in the next room that if they want to enjoy a day at the seaside they'd best hurry up, while there's still some seaside left. He thinks nothing of it, until a little later she lowers her voice to advise a passing acquaintance to sell her seaside apartment as soon as she can, unless she'd prefer a view of camels and palm trees and oases instead of the deep blue sea. She has it on good authority that the Mediterranean is fast disappearing.

Another group calls and Albert thinks it's time he took a hand, especially when it turns out that they own a boat presently moored in the marina at Lattes, just south of Montpellier. Eyes shining with prophetic zeal, Marie-Ange warns them of the dire consequences of delay. Jacques intervenes: Come off it, Marie-Ange, where did you get this drivel from?

It's not drivel, it's true, Marie-Ange says. Aristide said so, so there.

Jacques sighs deeply and explains that the time-scale isn't one that you can measure by the clock on the *mairie*. Marie-Ange takes some persuading. The Lattes boat-owners start to laugh. Marie-Ange gets agitated. Tears aren't far off.

The boat-owners leave and the storm breaks. Marie-Ange demands an apology from Jacques for showing her up in front of others. As you and I know, demanding an apology from someone hardly ever delivers the goods. How will this be resolved?

* * *

A few weeks later, on a perfect Sunday in mid-September, Le Choeur des Hauts Cantons has its annual choir outing to a hilltop chapel called St Hippolyte des Treize Vents, St Hippolyte of the Thirteen Winds, a name as picturesque as the place it identifies. The hills round here are usually steep sided and heavily wooded, but when you reach the top, having climbed through a notch or two of climate, they very often flatten out into an arable and pastoral landscape quite different from the almost sub-tropical terraced vineyards and cherry orchards in the valley hundreds of metres below. Indeed, I've known visiting aunts and suchlike, always slightly suspicious of our having come to live out here, comment 'Oh, it's just like Wales' or 'It reminds me of Berwickshire, up here', when we've taken them out for a drive. Clearly they draw great comfort from known quantities amid the alien corn we've chosen to exile ourselves in.

St Hippolyte was a ruin until an association was formed to restore it. Through badgering local authorities over a period of almost 30 years enough money was put together to undertake restoration, finding *maçons* to repair the stonework, *charpentiers* to replace the roof timbers of whole rough-hewn chestnut trunks, *carreleurs* to re-tile the floor and all the other trades needed to transform a derelict museum piece into a working centre of spiritual repose and self-discovery. It's now a beautiful chapel, standing in a clearing among the scented pinewoods, with a gîte for overnight stays and a communal kitchen and assembly room attached. Regular services aren't held here: there are no houses nearby and in any case the two local priests have 48 other places of worship to attend to between them. But it's a regular place of pilgrimage, and while we are up there several knots of pilgrims arrive, do whatever pilgims feel they have to do when they arrive at their journey's end, fill their water-bottles at the hand-cranked pump and depart. Beyond the chapel a path leads to a succession of wayside shrines and finally to a large hilltop cross, from which there are magnificent views across the valley towards the Espinouse mountains on the far side. If ever there was a place for reflection, coming to terms and acceptance, this is it.

The choir, however, has gone up there primarily to eat and drink, so the sopranos and altos set up trestle tables and plastic chairs borrowed from the gîte while the tenors and basses, following an immutable division of labour not always reflected in the kitchen at home, see to the lighting of the barbecue and the char-grilling of immense loops of Toulouse sausage. Jacques meanwhile is explaining to me in arguments fortified by a goodly *apéritif* of sangria that France's colonial and subsequent domestic history would have been very different if Marshal Leclerc hadn't been killed in an air crash in 1947. I'm quite happy to agree.

Sitting together a little further down the line of tables are Albert and Marie-Ange, and Jacques and Aristide too. All four are laughing and joking together, and clearly they've put their differences behind them. Wonderful. I don't know who was responsible for the reconciliation, but if it was measured, firmly fleshed out, sincere and unadulterated I suspect Albert's Quality Control hand was in it.

O Taste and see

I was splitting cherry logs a little way up the hill when an unfamiliar car drew up nearer the house. A smartly-dressed woman got out, picked her way across a shallow ditch and peered closely at a rotten tree stump.

Remembering that once during his madness George III had

stopped his carriage in Windsor Great Park in order to address an oak tree as the Prussian Ambassador, I resolved to react warily. I left my axe – I wouldn't have wanted to alarm her unduly – and came down the slope to ask if I could be of any help. It was most kind of me, she said in a polished Parisian accent. She was passing and had noticed a really splendid growth of fungi on the tree stump. Did I happen to know to whom they belonged?

I'd barely noticed them. There was indeed a magnificent cluster of nutbrown trumpetty mushrooms, like a half-buried brass band. I didn't know what they were. A sorry ignorance, of course, but every fungus under the sun grows round here, especially after a wet warm autumn. The exception is the truffle, which is the one we'd really appreciate. For us, identifying edible fungi is like learning the tango: to our shame we've just never got round to it, so we're incapable of sorting out the inedible ones from those we sniff at eagerly when someone else is frying them lightly in a little olive oil.

The upshot of all this was that I cut them away carefully, put them in a plastic bag and gave them to her. Certain now of her supper, she introduced herself as Angèle, thanked me effusively and in return invited us both to the next exhibition of her paintings. She had English friends in the area, we were bound to know them. She couldn't remember their names for the moment, but perhaps we could all come together?

* * *

Weeks later, just before Christmas, this invitation surfaced as unexpectedly as the mushrooms that gave rise to it. Some Anglo-Dutch friends rang to say they'd been invited to an art exhibition one Sunday. Would we join them? They understood we knew Angèle, the lady artist, too. So we went along, driving up and over the hills that separate our valley from the vineyard-carpeted Mediterranean plain.

It was a strange venue for an exhibition of paintings. After several wrong turns and stops to ask the way, we ran it to earth in a *Cave*

Biologique called Domaine de Lotantique. 'Cave' in this part of the world means a winery, a wine-producing unit. Usually they're housed in massive stone-built barns, but this one was in a modern concrete-block shed, all steel beams, insulated aluminium panels and enormous stainless steel wine-vats about the size of moonshot rockets.

The pictures were almost all wine-based: richly coloured, competent and painterly offerings of old Languedoc vintner's houses, vineyards, gnarled but fungus-free vine stumps, all owing much to Van Gogh and Cézanne and rather outshone by the gleaming sanitized pipes and spotless mirror-bright wine vats they were hung from. A couple of blotchy but shapely nudes were the exception, and even they were coloured in tones of *rouge, blanc* and *rosé*.

But of Angèle, the lady artist, there was no sign. A fleeting thought: surely the mushrooms I'd given her weren't poisonous? Ah, the proprietors Jean-Claude Crebassa and Elisa Riggio said, she'd gone to Mass, they'd try her mobile later. Meanwhile, would we like to sample the wines on offer? They were *Bio*, produced without inorganic fertilisers, weedkillers or pesticides.

* * *

Wine-tasting is the process known as *dégustation*, a rather unfortunate name for something that ought to be wholly pleasant. They pour a finger, maybe two, into a tall, concave glass. Then it's over to you. Here's the drill, or one of them: no two wine-tasters will follow exactly the same pattern, and devoted partisans of one or other method may even come to blows.

1. If you're serious about this, make certain that the bottle of white or *rosé* has been so freshly opened that condensation forms on the bottle. The red, however, should have been opened some time, enough for it to have taken on the ambient temperature. If the *dégustation* leads to a worthwhile order, they'll sometimes re-cork the sample bottle for you temporarily and include it in your order free of charge.

2. Hold the glass to the light. If the wine is murky, like cabbage-water, it probably tastes like it, too. If it's aflame with all the glorious clarity and colour of a sun-filtered stained glass window, move on happily to step 3.

3. If it's a red you're trying, cup the glass in your hand, tilt it from side to side, swirl the wine about gently without sloshing it. Take your time. Watch the trace it leaves. Is it dribble-free, silky and unbroken? You could be on to a winner. Cruise confidently on to step 4, your nose a-twitch.

   If you've opted for white or *rosé*, hold the glass by the stem. Both are at their best when drunk cold, but how cold is a matter of personal taste. Temperature is all. As a general guide whites and especially *rosés* won't be at their best if they're too warm for condensation to form on the outside of the glass. If your glass mists up, you're on the right track. You won't get very much out of Stage 4 and can skip joyfully to Stage 5.

4. The slight warmth of your hand through the glass should help to release the bouquet: test the fragrance firstly in one long, gentle inhalation, and then in a series of delicate, barely perceptible snifflets. When you've fully drawn breath, hold it there for a second or two. You should find the upper reaches of your nostrils and sinuses being very agreeably teased, giving you an idea of how you'll feel when you've drunk a glass or two. If you're a smoker, however, this experience will probably be completely abortive.

5. This is it. Take a small mouthful. Let it lie on the tongue for a moment. Then move it about in your mouth. Burgundy wine-tasters filter it to and fro between their lower teeth, an unappealing action called *la grumée* designed to keep the wine near the tip of the tongue. Don't feel obliged to do this, but different parts of the tongue will react differently to build up your appreciation of the

spectrum of flavours. Finally swallow it. Don't spit it out in any circumstances. (I write this under the assumption that you're not going to drink so much that you're going to end up under the table.) Don't take another mouthful until the aftertaste has disappeared, like the final glow of a beautiful sunset giving way to night. Ah.

6. Clear your palate before the next sample with water or something neutral like a piece of bread. Good *dégustations* will provide bread, or perhaps a bland cheese or not too spicy sausage. Beware the *dégustation* where the palate-clearers are highly flavoured: it's done deliberately to mask the inferior quality of the wine. A really determined *dégustateur* can turn the experience into a modest lunch.

In due course we left, the heavier by a dozen or so bottles. The reds were good, but the whites, especially one called Galinette, were particularly impressive. I'm afraid we didn't buy any of Angèle's paintings. Why look at the pictures when you can drink the wine? On second thoughts, though, those nudes . . .

Back to school

I could have refused, I suppose, but the headmistress was so appealing in her very French way, all smiles, dimples and fluttered eyelids. When I said I'd think about it she gave me *la bise*, the kiss on both cheeks, and that was that, really: how could I say no? After all, when were you last kissed by a headmistress?

Mardi prochain, alors? she said. You can start next Tuesday, then? I said yes, and went home to worry about teaching music in a French school. A bit of a revolution. Probably very salutary, casting aside the mantle of a time-hardened headmaster to become the lowest of the low, the comic foreign music teacher. (Admittedly, this was three or four years further on.) Anyway, in for a centime, in for a euro, in for Madame's irresistible lure-o, and the following Tuesday I parked in front of St Pons cathedral and wandered off through the maze of narrow streets and cobbled alleys of the old quarter and presently rang the bell at an undistinguished door giving no hint of what lay beyond.

Inside it was unexpectedly spacious, with bright and airy classrooms, a large central playground, a garden with trees and shrubs and children's vegetable patches, and an open verandah for summer shade and winter shelter. No such thing as that abomination of Scottish primary schools, the wet playtime, notorious for cooped-up energies, petty misdeeds and steamed-up windows. (Indeed, in Scotland once a 9-year-old called Nabil, a lad with reading difficulties, was sent to me to be disciplined because he'd written **SEX** in large letters with his finger on the window during one wet playtime. Suppressing a smile, the maverick in me was tempted to say well done, Nabil, here's a gold star: not only was his spelling perfect, he'd had the wit to write the word backwards, so that it could be read for maximum effect from outside, and a little praise does wonders with slow pupils. But Nabil's class teacher had to be backed up too . . . Suppose parents saw the offending word? And what about the cleaners? Fingers on windows leave abiding traces . . . in fact the whole matter was so stuffed to bursting with pedagogical implications that I sometimes used it afterwards as an initiative test in teacher interviews. Thank you, Nabil.)

I knocked gently at a classroom door and found myself among the infants. They stood up, very politely, all except the very tiny ones, busy in their own little world. Madame la Directrice, the head teacher, shook my hand and introduced me as *Monsieur Chreestophair*, who had come to teach them music. 'Campbell', she explained to me, was a name only familiar to whisky drinkers – a blend called Clan Campbell is a leading brand here – not a common phenomenon in primary schools. 'Howes', bristling with un-French Hs and Ws and 'ow' sounds, is quite beyond most French children, let alone adults, to get their vocal chords round. *Chreestophair* was much simpler.

I was due to start with *les grands*, the big ones – there were only two classes, about 50 children altogether – so she took me to their classroom and introduced me to Chantal, a teacher in her late 20s dressed in *un jogging* (a kind of shell suit) and *les baskets* (trainers, what you play basketball in). Most of the children were dressed in jogging and baskets too, a bit of a surprise for one who'd spent his professional life surrounded by kids in uniform. A dangerous informality, gnawing at the very roots of school discipline? Not at all: there was deep silence, hardly a scrape of chair on wooden floor as the children stood up when I came in. I asked them what they knew about Scotland, so they told me about the mountains, the castles, the Loch Ness Monster and . . . the ghosts. People here are convinced Scotland is hyper-haunted, goodness knows why. The children knew France had been trounced by Scotland at rugby at Murrayfield a few days before, but there was no bounce, no we'll-show-you-next-time; France hadn't played well, and please would I teach them *O Flower of Scotland*?

Chantal said they wanted to sing me a song they'd learnt, in English. If their singing was as good as their manners, listening would be a pleasure. A girl called Jennifer (English names are fashionable here: call your child Kévin – with accent – and he should go far) said the song was called, apparently, *Oo enzie seun shans*. I nodded non-committally. *Un, deux, trois*, a sharp intake of breath, and they were off. You never heard such a wild caterwauling. It soon became obvious why Madame la Directrice had been so keen to recruit me. These kids had never had a music lesson in their lives. There was work to be done. No desperate hurry: the next France-Scotland match wouldn't be until the following January or February. Time enough to get *O Flower of Scotland* up to scratch, and maybe to work out what *Oo enzie seun shans* was supposed to mean.

Picture the scene: it's a year and more later, and the backdrop is the magnificent altarpiece in St Pons Cathedral, rising like a wedding cake in the local pink and white marble, polished and glittering with a thousand candles, crowned by the famous organ, its columns of gilded pipes spread like a fabulous giant bird with wings outstretched, about to take its majestic flight into the vast vaulted spaces that dwindle away into the distant gloom by the east door.

They stand in front of the stepped marble altar balustrade in two or three neat rows, jogging and baskets no longer but a bow tie here, a gingham dress there, posh frocks, best jeans, bright eyes and shining hair, Charlotte, Anthony, Pierre-Luc, Sandra, Anaïs, Jérôme, Clément, Hamed, Léa and all the rest. There's a hush, the last fidget and rustle from the audience dies away, *un, deux,* a sharp intake of breath and off they go:

> *O floo-er of Scotland!*
> *Ou-enn ou-eel ou-ee see your lahk a-gain?*
> *. . . ou-ee bit 'ill an' glen . . .*
> *. . . prood Edward's ar-mee . . .*
> *. . . an' sent zem 'ome-ou-ard . . .*
> *. . . to sink again.*

Cameras flash, the last echo dies. Furious applause. *O Flower of Scotland* is well practised, having been on the stocks for some months, since the start of the annual Six Nations rugby tournament. Whatever the merits of a folk-type song of no great antiquity, it lodged firmly in one young breast: on the day of the France-Scotland match Emilie, a bright and smiling 10-year-old without the least interest in rugby, said to her father 'Papa, when the match starts, call me in from the garden; I want to sing the Scottish hymn with them'. And so she did. It's arguable that she and her pals know the words at least as well as the average Murrayfield terraceman.

And now here they were singing it in public. It was a good concert, quite an occasion, with two choirs and a string orchestra taking a breather while the children performed. A full house, too, as there usually is if children are taking part. I had some doubts about their next song, *What shall we do with the drunken sailor?* You can never be too careful with these things, you never know whose ecclesiastical susceptibilities you might offend with mention of strong drink in a place of worship, although the chances of finding any English-speakers here are about as remote finding sailors in a condition to walk straight down a white line while enunciating 'ecclesiastical susceptibilities' to the St Pons *gendarmerie*. So it was discreetly shortened on the programme to *What shall we do?* which I felt sounded enough like a request for Guidance from Above to pass muster in the cathedral.

So the children have increased their English vocabularies no end, with words like *hooray*, *long-boat*, *scuppers* and *hosepipe*. Maybe these words have a limited scope in a small country town whose only connection with the sea is the Friday evening oyster stall opposite the Café des Sports, and the usefulness factor wasn't much increased by the next song, *Un éléphant peu réticent*, A Noisy Elephant. But at least the ghost of *Oo enzie seun shans* had been decently laid. You've twigged, of course, which is more than I did for a long time: When the sun shines . . .

Breaking and entering

4.20am. The bedside telephone rings. Panic, panic. What disaster's this? Who's died? It's strange how your first thoughts are those of catastrophe when you're woken from sleep in the early hours.

In fact it's an alarm company telling us that the security of Claude's and Béatrice's house has been compromised. Claude and Béatrice are an elderly couple who live a few hundred metres away down the lane. They asked us once if they could give our telephone number to the alarm company as the first contact if anything went wrong: they'd feel so much more secure whenever they went away, having set the alarm system, if they knew there was someone on hand to take charge. In a weak moment we agreed. If we'd realised the full implications, we would have had second thoughts.

The alarm company installed a system of electronic security seals on window and door shutters and linked it to the house telephone. The telephone was programmed to call the alarm company several times every 24 hours, in relation to periods statistically proved to be preferred by house-breakers. If it failed to call at any of the pre-programmed times, it would mean that a security seal had been broken: the duty officer would ring the nominated neighbours, viz. ourselves. We would really have preferred them not to ask.

And now here was the alarm company ringing us in the early hours. Strange. Claude and Béatrice hadn't said they were going away. They must have forgotten to tell us.

Bundle into old clothes and bedroom slippers. Find torch and mobile. Preset number to 17 for the police, the French equivalent of 999 in the UK. Get in car, quietly drive the 400 metres to neighbour's house. Park ready for quick getaway if necessary. It's a bright moonlit night. Oh goodness, there's a car parked by the house, where Claude usually parks. Should I phone the police now? Staying in the shadows, I approach the car. Local registration. I feel the exhaust: it's cold. H'm. How do I account for this? I creep round the house, shining my torch at shuttered windows and testing doors, expecting a masked and hooded villain to jump out at me any second, brandishing what the French call *une matraque*, i.e. a cosh. I can't explain what imbecile idiocy led us to accept Claude's and Béatrice's nomination as the first line of defence.

Then . . . it occurs to me that the car with the cold exhaust may actually be Claude's, and that in fact they're in the house tucked up in bed, where I ought to be. Maybe they're lying there, quaking, barely daring to breathe, whispering:

Claude: *O my God, wake up! Wake up! Listen! There's somebody creeping round outside: I can hear them trying the doors. It's burglars!*

Béatrice: *Well, go and have a look, then.*

Claude: *No, you.*

Béatrice: *What do you mean, me?*

Claude: *I've got a bad leg, don't forget.*

Béatrice: *Bed lag, more like.* [I don't know how this would work in French, I confess.] *I'm not going, I don't want to be knocked on the head.*

Claude: *Hold on, hold on a minute: why don't you go and phone the police while I put some clothes on?*

Béatrice: *Keep your voice down, for goodness' sake . . . Listen, they're right outside. Look, that's their torches shining through the crack in the shutters. There must be half a dozen of them. We'll all be murdered in our beds. Do something, for God's sake . . .*

And by this time I've persuaded myself that the best thing I can possibly do is to creep home and see how things are in the morning. When I get in Josephine has made a cup of tea. Wonderful. Somehow we're wide awake. We talk about break-ins, agreeing that they're mercifully few in this part of the world.

* * *

Several years ago, regular journeys took me past a lonely holiday house up on the Col de Broussette. A handwritten notice appeared outside one day saying *ATTENTION CAMBRIOLEURS* (Burglars, take note) and which claimed that the house had been done over 5 times already and there was nothing of the slightest value left inside. Passing a few weeks later I noticed that someone had crossed out the 5 and had replaced it with a 6.

Still later a 7 appeared in place of the 6 together with the comment *cé vré,* I suppose a disappointed housebreaker's attempt at writing *c'est vrai,* it's true. I don't know how far submitting suspects to spelling tests forms part of French police investigation procedures, but they should have picked up this chap by the time they got to Question 2.

Unless it was all a bluff, of course. Marcel Pagnol, the Thomas Hardy of Provence, makes one of his characters in *Manon des Sources*, the sly and sordid Ugolin Soubeyran, pin a notice to his kitchen cupboard which says:

CABRIOLEUR, ANTENTION!
Vous fatigez pas à sercher l'arjent. Elle est pas ici. Elle est à la Banque,
au milieu d'Aubagne, à côté de la jeandarmerie. 12 Cour Voltère.
Y a rien à faire.

(Burglar, take notice!
Don't bother looking for money. It isn't here. It's in the Bank, in the centre of Aubagne, beside the police station, 12 Cours Voltaire.
You're wasting your time here.)

Spelling and grammar don't appear to have been Ugolin's strong points, but the irony of the situation was that, true to French peasant tradition, he kept his stash of *louis d'or* in a pot under a hearthstone. Although his unrequited love for Manon robbed him of his heart, his five wits and eventually his life, his gold remained intact. Ugolin reckoned it was mention of the police station next door to the bank that deterred burglars, but clearly *Manon des Sources* was never a set book up at the Col de Broussette.

* * *

Then there was the pure farce at Mousse les Grieux. In an effort to spread the police budget a little further, the story went, the authorities came out with proposals to close down the *gendarmerie* and to transfer its staff to the purpose-built police station at St Amans Soult several kilometres further down the valley. As always when anyone tries to tamper with the status quo there was outcry, demonstrations, petitions and all the usual paraphernalia of public outrage, and as a result the village was allowed to keep its *gendarmerie*, a fine 19th-century mini-château with handsome wrought iron gates.

Some time later a Madame Bot, an elderly lady who lived in the first-floor flat across the street from the bank, was disturbed in the early hours by the sounds of crowbar on hinge and high-speed drill on cash dispenser. She peeped across the road and saw several hooded villains breaking into the bank. Living in the flat alone, she tiptoed to the telephone and summoned the immediate aid of Mousse's noble police brigade. She drew up a chair to the window to watch the unfolding drama through a gap in the shutters.

In vain. Minutes passed, five, ten, fifteen. No police, although the *gendarmerie* is all of two minutes' stroll from the bank. After 20 undisturbed minutes the swag-laden villains roared off. She rang the gendarmerie again, boiling over with anguish and frustration. Why hadn't they reacted to her first call?

'We can't get out, Madame,' an exasperated *gendarme* replied. 'The robbers chained and padlocked the *gendarmerie* gates on their way to the bank . . . '

Maybe she needn't have worried too much. A day or two later one of the villains was caught passing counterfeit notes, and I don't expect his defence that the bank had furnished them in the first place carried much weight. In any case he peached on the others and for all I know they're still slopping out in what the French call *le bagne* or *la taule*, which you could translate as jug, clink, stir, chokey or the slammer. Take your pick, as they used to say to Dartmoor inmates on hard labour.

* * *

So these villains can't have been the same as the ones who, having identified another isolated and unoccupied holiday house as easy meat, chose a wild and stormy November night to do the place over, trusting that the local *flics*, i.e. the cops, the Bill, PC Plod or Insp. Knacker, would be tucked up in their beds.

Up the drive they rumbled in their stolen white van while above their heads the storm raged. They backed up to the house, broke in, relieved the Dutch owners of fridge, microwave, television, video and anything else with any value in the back streets of the nearest large town. But nature intervened: while they were helping themselves, an oak tree as ancient as it was huge blew down, falling across the drive and preventing any gang of villains not equipped with chainsaws, blocks, tackles and tractors from showing a clean pair of rear lights. What they did is anybody's guess, but some weeks later, when the Dutch owners turned up for Christmas, they were very surprised to find that someone had made them a present of not only several winters' firewood but also quite a decent white van, inexplicably full of their electrical goods. Nature just occasionally does redress the balance in favour of the deserving.

* * *

We've finished our tea by the time we've swapped these stories. We go back to bed to recapture what's left of a broken night. In the morning I try to ring Claude, but the line's engaged. A tiny suspicion enters my mind. I go down to see what's doing at his house, and I find him watering his lawn. Clearly nothing untoward has happened, and I'm quite relieved. I tell him the tale of the night's adventures and he's horrified. He invites me to follow him indoors to check the telephone line. It's only then that he discovers that whoever last used the telephone the evening before hadn't replaced it correctly.

So I got abject apologies and Josephine got a lovely bunch of flowers. I'm sure it's a privilege to be so trusted by one's neighbours, but it's a privilege we're more than happy to share with anybody else.

Doctor, doctor

There's a mid-morning tap at the window. We look up from the milky instant coffee we've never quite abandoned in favour of the French mini-cups, hot and strong, and we're pleased to see our doctor, Agnès, with a large cardboard box in her arms.

Agnès is young, attractive and cheerful, the sort of person who makes you feel better just by looking at her. Just what the doctor ordered, in fact. She and her farmer husband Colin are building a house a little further up the lane. Not personally, of course: her hands-on activity extends to pulses and dislocated thumbs and soothing the fevered brow, but not to bricks and mortar. No, M. Panafieu the *maçon* from the next village and his happy band whistle and sing from morn till night, when they're not trembling in their boots, because Agnès, when provoked, has a fiery temper and a tongue spiced with oaths anything but Hippocratic: woe betide any builder who leaves nailheads showing or dollops of *crépi* (i.e rendering) lying about. Indeed, there's a French proverb *On connaît le maçon par le pied du mur*, you can judge the builder by the foot of the wall. How M. Panafieu rates on the *crépi*-dollop scale I don't know, but the house is going up slowly, and by the time Agnès has moved in and has become our nearest neighbour I might actually have got round to telling you what was in the box she was carrying.

Well, it was meat. Prime cuts of lean beef, vacuum-wrapped and labelled according to the French *traçabilité* system, so that you can tell exactly where the animal came from, when it was slaughtered and all the other details needed to reassure a country – indeed, a continent – shaken by various food scares that their beef is safe.

We were rather surprised. It's not every day that your doctor appears on the doorstep with a gift of enough prime beef to keep you going for two or three months. There's no market for her husband's cattle just now, she explains; it's cheaper for him to slaughter his beasts and give the meat away than to keep on feeding them. It's an ill wind . . . and I can't think of any better guarantee of its quality than your own doctor's endorsement.

* * *

I wonder if Marie-Odile would have done the same? She was another lady doctor I'd had a few years earlier, wirier and tougher than Agnès but no less attractive, in a *gamine* sort of way. To Marie-Odile I went once, after a spell in a Toulouse cardiac unit, to consult her about a low-cholesterol diet. (The damage to my arteries had been done in Scotland, not France: locust years of over-indulgence in pipe tobacco and school canteen deep-fried jam doughnuts and custard had finally caught up.) A-tremble with expectations of a life sentence to bread and water, I sat down in her surgery under the spell of her blue eyes and wheaten hair while she listed the items *à privilégier*, poultry, fish, fruit, vegetables, pasta and so on with such an engaging smile that it was easy to promise to lay off animal fats, eggs and most dairy products including my beloved cheeses just to please her. I expect piecrust was on her list too, but I have to say that fancying your doctor across the consulting room desk really does encourage you to do what you're told.

But suddenly, as though she'd divined this thought, her manner changed into its chilled steel mode: '*STOP sucreries!*' she said sharply, and wrote it down. I sighed. Heigh ho. No more sweets, jams, custards, puds, chocs, all that. Well, fair enough. No real problem, I supposed; the French consume a tiny fraction of such things compared with the sweet-toothed, sugar-addicted Anglo-Saxons.

Then the real blow came. '*STOP alcohol!*' she ordered, as though she was a dormitory prefect (oh! wild thought!) who had caught me pillow-fighting. 'No alcohol. Give it up. No more.'

Night suddenly fell, a black night of agony and anguish unparalleled in gloom since the lovely Gillian turned me down all those years ago . . .

. . . but Marie-Odile was still speaking, honeyed words of comfort and joy: 'Yes, wine with each meal, of course, that goes without saying. And maybe a finger of whisky at night to help your circulation. But otherwise cut it right out.'

Marie-Odile was loved throughout her parish. And rightly so. I don't expect you ever became a doctor, did you, Gillian?

* * *

This refreshing attitude to wine was underlined during that selfsame stay in the excellent Clinique Pasteur in Toulouse having a coronary artery reamed. The lunch trolley would trundle down the corridor shortly after midday, and a clinking of plates and cutlery would precede a discreet tap at the door. In would come an attendant bearing a tray with the day's special, *salade niçoise* followed by *colin à l'oseille* or whatever, and invariably there would be a 25cl bottle of *rouge* to help it down.

A private clinic, the Clinique Pasteur? Not at all. It was all on the French national health system. Little wonder the usual French toast is *Santé!* Good health!

Something to get your teeth into

I expect it's happened to you, although I wouldn't wish it on anyone: you're scrubbing away, the toothbrush loaded with Parogencyl (well, that's the toothpaste we have here: it's presumably on sale in the UK too, because the tube's inscribed in both languages, which is as useful for brushing up your French as it is for your teeth) and suddenly there's a deep sense of unease as something solid goes rattling down the plug-hole. You poke about gingerly with the tip of your tongue and discover that you've lost *un plombage*, a filling, and it's no joke.

140

Pierre, our ever-accommodating dentist, was happy to slip me into his appointments schedule, and forty-five minutes later I was in his waiting room idly looking at a weekly magazine. *Le Personnage de l'Année*, the cover said, The Personality of the Year, and instead of a photo-montage of all the people it might have been there was a polished square of reflective foil. Just the thing for baring the teeth into for a last-minute inspection . . . and there was Pierre calling me into his spotless surgery. Ten minutes later I was patched up pending something more permanent, but not before he had commented favourably on the dental work done some years before in Scotland.

When it comes to dentists unwinding, my Scottish dentist used to spend his spare time piloting light aircraft and playing in a big band. Pierre unwinds by going fishing, not that he has to go very far because his house is perched on a rocky outcrop just above the river, so in theory in he doesn't have to do much more than hang his line out of the window and haul them in. Some lines from Robert Browning commend this diversity:

> *. . . a butcher paints,*
> *A baker rhymes for his pursuit,*
> *Candlestick-maker much acquaints*
> *His soul with song, or, haply mute,*
> *Blows out his brains upon the flute.*

In the mid-90s I worked closely with Eudes Gély, the dentist in Mousse les Grieux. Our business hadn't much to do with teeth. Eudes was writing an opera, and wanted help with the rules of harmony and the basic grammar of composition. He must have heard I'd arranged one or two gospel songs for the St Pons choir, a slender qualification for in-depth involvement in the vast sweep of Eudes' conception. During our first, tentative meetings he outlined his project, an opera on the theme of Prometheus on a scale so gigantic that it dwarfed Wagner's *Ring* cycle. He wanted something like five simultaneous stages, one of which was to be an ice-rink, plus a cyclorama and an orchestra pit. There was no libretto, just a beautifully produced draft scenario. Most of the music was already written, a multitude of disparate pieces conceived within his limited keyboard technique at his synthesiser. Some pieces, in someone else's writing, had been professionally arranged for piano, and indeed Eudes gave me two of his CDs, recorded by a more able pianist. I asked him who had made these arrangements, who had gone to the extraordinary ant-hill labour of transcribing his basic sketches into playable piano music. Ah, he said, *c'était une sainte*, she was a saint. Clearly all this had cost money. It turned out that he had his own recording studio near Montpellier, complete with a Steinway grand piano, a studio which had been designed and built largely with the realisation of his opera in mind. The mystery deepened: if Eudes had such means at his disposal, what was he doing practising as a dentist?

The upshot of all this was that once a week, on his free afternoon, I dusted off student memories of the innards of music like ritornello form and Neapolitan sixths and spent a couple of hours with him, taking his pieces apart, working on them and putting them back together again.

He wasn't an easy pupil. He wasn't terribly interested in what I had to teach him. Maybe it didn't meet his needs: what he really wanted was another donkey-work saint who would write the words of his opera, set them to his music and arrange it all for voices and orchestra. Incentives were proposed. One of them was an expenses-paid trip to the United States: once the Prologue to Prometheus had been fleshed out and the music recorded, we should go together to Los Angeles to find backers. I'm afraid I declined, guiltily aware that I was adding one more layer of frustration to one whose conceptions outran his capabilities. Besides, he was buying ever more sophisticated software designed to do the hack work. Unsurprisingly, our relationship didn't really prosper and we gradually drifted apart, a separation maybe hastened when he came to supper one evening: without warning or provocation the cat, normally a byword for heavy-lidded sluggishness, suddenly attacked him and drew blood.

Driving through Mousse les Grieux some time after this very embarrassing incident, I was surprised to see *local à louer* (premises to let) on the door of his surgery. He'd often mentioned that he would like to give up his practice in order to concentrate on his music. Evidently he'd grasped the nettle. It was even more surprising a year or two later to receive an invitation headed *Eudes Gély, compositeur*, i.e. composer. We were invited to the Renaissance Rooms in the heart of Montpellier to be present at the champagne launch of a CD of his music, recently recorded in the Abbey Road studios by the London Symphony Orchestra. Saints had been at work. Was this the big time?

So we found ourselves among forty or fifty of Montpellier's glitterati listening to an hour's worth of New Age-ish music called *Renouvellement de l'éternité* interpreted by a solo dancer whose figure was such a distraction from my concentrated listening for any vestigial trace of anything I'd ever taught Eudes that I was happy enough to slouch in the back row, her gyrations unseen. I couldn't spot anything, however, not even a Neapolitan sixth.

We drove home, leaving Eudes and his business manager Hubert about to set off for California in search of saints, angels and more champagne launches. There was much to speculate on. Probably the real story behind all this was the bond between creator and enabler, between Eudes and his backer, but for a composer to have got this length was pretty terrific. For a dentist, it was absolutely astonishing. Maybe Eudes too had looked at the cover of the magazine I found in Pierre's waiting room? Crown him with many crowns, is all I can say about him and his achievements. Just what Pierre told me ought to be done to replace my lost fillings, too.

Pièce de Résistance

I'd been asked to bring the rehearsal of my choir, Le Chœur des Hauts Cantons, to an early finish, about 9.45, to allow them to celebrate Epiphany, which lasts for about three weeks here. There's nothing very religious about it. Like so many festivals rooted in the church calendar it's more to do with filling the tum.

No social or corporate gathering in January is complete without *le gâteau des rois*, a circular bun sprinkled with coloured sugar. Up-market Epiphany buffs may get theirs in puff pastry and *à la frangipane*, with almond paste, but either way one of the segments has a *fève* hidden in it, usually a china favour. The lucky finder announces the discovery joyfully – if he/she hasn't broken a tooth on it – and gets to wear the paper crown included in the pack. It's unthinkable, of course, to nibble at your segment of *le gâteau des rois* without some lubrication, so the choir got through several bottles of Blanquette de Limoux, a sort of country cousin of champagne, and Jacquot (pron. 'zhacko'), one of the tenors and a clog-wearing shepherd, won the crown with his teeth intact and cycled home wearing it.

A week later Edmond Dougados, longest-serving of the basses, asked for the early cut-off for another celebration, by no means an everyday one. After 57 years of refusal he'd finally decided to accept *la médaille militaire* he'd been cited for while fighting for the Resistance in 1944. Not even going to Paris to receive his decoration from the hands of the President would give him as much pleasure as fêting his beloved choir in real champagne. So the corks popped and the bubbles winked and the laughter pealed and we all felt very proud of having a Resistance hero in our midst even if it had taken us half a century to realise it.

In due course, about the time of the 60th anniversary of D-Day,

Edmond produced a remarkable CD which someone had put together for him. It contained the documentary and photographic records of his Resistance activities.

The liberation of France from Nazi occupation in 1944 was helped immeasurably by the Resistance. It's a debt that's impossible to calculate. The actions of the Resistance are by now woven inextricably into the French national consciousness, I think particularly in the Midi. After occupying the north of France in 1940, the Nazis ostensibly allowed the south of France to look after its own domestic affairs, with an administration set up in Vichy, a town in the Allier *département* known mainly for its natural springs until Marshal Pétain established a pro-Nazi puppet government there. In November 1942 Nazi and Fascist Italian troops moved in to occupy southern France too.

What swelled the numbers of the French Resistance in the south, sometimes called the *maquis,* was the universal imposition of the *Service Obligatoire de Travail,* shortened to STO, by which all men not employed in reserved occupations were required to register for work for the Nazis in Germany or elsewhere. This was virtually slave labour, and it's hardly surprising that thousands of young Frenchmen simply disappeared and went underground rather than sign on for the STO.

Among them was Edmond, then a young weaver in the Tarn *département.* Summoned to register with the STO, he and several friends slipped away into the impenetrable forests of the Montagne Noire. They gave themselves code-names: Edmond called himself Le Zed (French for the letter Z) because when you reversed his first name and surname it sounded like 'Dougados-Edmond', with the sound 'zed' hidden inside it, a subterfuge baffling enough to his intimates let alone to any Gestapo investigators.

The southern Resistance was beginning to organise itself, supplied mainly by the British. Le Zed and his friends tried to join various embryo units, but found it difficult: no one trusted anyone, denunciation was endemic, some saw membership of the Resistance as an opportunity to settle personal scores, the Vichy government wasn't universally despised, some actually welcomed the Nazi occupation. Rather than harbour possible traitors to the general movement, it was sometimes more expedient to encourage small bands of Resistance fighters to operate independently, with freedom to attack the enemy as and when possible. By 1944 Le Zed and his ten-odd comrades in arms had formed themselves into a CFL, a *Corps Franc de Libération*, under the loose control of the Tarn Resistance command, and so began the headiest days of his life.

The group really came into its own after D-Day, as the Nazi troops occupying the south were called to reinforce the embattled forces in Normandy. Groups like Le Zed's CFL harried them every step of the way: his citations mention fire-fights in remote farms, ambushes, sabotage, assaults in force on staging camps, the 'cleansing' of Toulouse of *miliciens*, pro-Nazi police. The transcribed oral accounts include the meting out of local summary justice: collaborators ('*collabos*') with the authorities beaten up and mutilated; a suspected informer executed by firing squad; a factory-owner promised the same fate if he didn't pay his workers within 24 hours (we're not told the outcome of this); requisitions of food, vehicles, petrol and particularly cigarettes, and we don't know if they were ever paid for. Cruel times.

The photographs are particularly fascinating. The summer of 1944 was hot, to judge by the bare torsos of fit and healthy young men exercising on improvised shooting ranges, draped over the bonnets of their requisitioned Citroën *tractions avant*, a car familiar from Maigret films, requisitioned cigarettes drooping from their lips, British-parachuted side arms at the ready. The 22-year-old Le Zed, neat and soldierly, looks out proudly, conscious of the strength of camaraderie, but hardly of the heroic qualities he will be vested with later.

Edmond is elderly now, and apart from his CD the only record of

Le Zed is a dog-eared typewritten slip of paper in his pocket book listing the code-names of his CFL comrades, Albert, Zazou, Bruno and the others. Some have been crossed out as mortality has caught up with them, but the memory of those heady days of 1944, for all that they only lasted a few months, has never left him. It's given to few of us to have experienced the danger, the adventure, the excitement, the sharp-edged team mentality, under the umbrella of an intense patriotism and the sense that one is really doing something very important for one's country. I leave Le Zed with his transcribed account of the announcement of the D-Day landings:

> The landings have started, at least that's what Albert heard just now on Radio Vichy. But we don't have the details and nothing is certain. So we're all there gathered round the radio, mad with impatience and excited to the highest pitch, when it packs up. However Zazou listened to the BBC broadcast in English, which confirmed what we already knew.
>
> So what joy, what immense joy . . . what delight in this house where everything was mournful and sad: suddenly everything is happy, we're happy to be alive . . . sure, a wave of sadness swept over us at the thought of our comrades, our friends who have been killed. They too waited for this news, but we, the terrorists [he actually uses the word *terroristes*], the *maquisards* know that they will be avenged.'

But why did Edmond have to wait 57 years before claiming his medal? Deep waters stir here, ancient anathemas swirl up. He had to wait until a fellow *maquisard* died, someone to whom he had certain obligations. I don't know what they were. Ask Edmond and he says something vague about General de Gaulle. I should think you're about as likely to discover the truth now as as you are to find a *fève* in your *gâteau des rois*.

Mediterranean delights

Summer and winter, early every Wednesday and Friday evening we're interrupted in whatever we're doing by a mighty noise from somewhere down in the village, a tidal wave of gibberish, and there's no excuse for missing M. Maigre, the travelling fishmonger. At least, gibberish it seemed to me when I first came to live in Olargues, but bi-weekly repetition has taught me that if I sit up, listen carefully and pay close attention, always salutary things for an ex-headmaster to do, some sense can be made of it. Maybe it doesn't matter much; after all, there are few meaningful insights to be had from the sound your alarm clock makes, it's enough that it makes a noise at the right time. The medium is the message, and our only doubt is whether, if M. Maigre is reaching the end of his round, his van isn't furnished with more decibels than fish.

Anyway, I've learnt to pick out a few words, although I'm still not exactly certain how they're strung together: *Eh bé, je viens d'arriver* (OK, I've just arrived) . . . *seiche* . . . *baudroie* . . . *merlan* . . . *rascasse* . . . *rouget* . . . *l'océan* . . . *la mer.* The ever-knowledgeable Josephine tells me that *l'océan* refers to fish from the Atlantic and *la mer* to fish from the Mediterranean, a reminder that it isn't really very far away and that we should go more often.

It's not really very far. An hour's journey over the hills and down across the vineyard-covered plain, and there it is, sparkling in the sun, wavelets lapping the unbroken sands that stretch for kilometre after kilometre from the Camargue to the stub-end of the Pyrenees and the Spanish border: the Mediterranean, cradle of western civilisation. A Latin teacher of mine once advanced twin theories that the spread of western civilisation around the Mediterranean basin was due to the Phoenicians' endless inshore search for the murex, the shellfish that gave the costly and rare Imperial purple dye, while the absence of tides, bar a centimetre or two, made cape-to-cape navigation and overnight beaching so much easier than in the tidal oceans.

Tucked up in our valley we forget that it's there, in winter. In summer there are strong tides, but of a different kind: the daily ebb and flow of waves of people reaching ever closer to the water's edge as the day warms up, retreating as the sun goes down, leaving a tideline of churned-up sand, crumbs and buried *mégots*, fag-ends. We forget the toe-scorching sands, the sweating ice-cream and Orangina sellers, the microlights trailing advertising streamers, the scanty to non-existent beachwear that doesn't owe much to the murex but drags middle-aged observers like me uncomfortably back to lost opportunities of their youth.

But that's all months away. On a perfect winter's day, clear and cloudless, we chose a spot, warm in the low January sun, between the ancient Greek colony of Agde and the port of Sète. There's a narrow sand-bar linking the two, carrying the road parallel with the railway line from Montpellier to Barcelona between the sea and the lagoon behind, a shallow inland sea called l'Etang de Thau. We chose a parking spot from the thousands on offer, let Bellamy the golden retriever out – dogs aren't encouraged in summer – and ambled down after her to the water's edge.

The beach was deserted, not a Phoenician winkle-picker, topless girl or Latin teacher in sight. We wondered what a far-out fishing boat was hauling in, and whether the catch would turn up the next day in M. Maigre's van and we would hear his mighty voice announcing that he'd just arrived and that *la mer* had yielded up *seiche* (cuttlefish) . . . *baudroie* (monkfish) . . . *merlan* (whiting) . . . *rouget* (red mullet) . . . and *rascasse*. *Rascasse* is a fearsomely ugly fish that has no English equivalent, the sort of creature from the depths that gives other fish and small children the night terrors, and which is much valued for the famous Mediterranean fish stew (it's not really a soup), *bouillabaisse*.

M. Maigre is as keen to dispense recipes for his fish as he is to sell them, but he's cagey about *bouillabaisse*. However he'll oblige, with the proviso that you're likely to get as many different recipes as people you ask, and, since it's a dish from Marseilles, and as the Marseillais are very protective of their own, his version risks being elbowed into the *Vieux Port* on a dark night with no lifebelts handy. It all depends what fish are available. A real *bouillabaisse*, the sort of thing you can imagine Marcel Pagnol's Marseilles quayside characters tucking into, will indeed include the famous *rascasse*, head and all, *baudroie* and *merlan*, but M. Maigre's stock stops short of other fresh-caught fish like *grondin* (gurnard), *vive* (weever or stargazer) and *congre* (conger eel), which should be cleaned in sea-water and then boiled up long and fierce in a broth of olive oil, water, onions, tomatoes, seasoning and the indispensable saffron. Some of the fish will disintegrate, others can be pulled out more or less whole and laid on a plate to be served beside bowls of broth into which rafts of garlic-rubbed toast have been launched. Immediacy is all.

If I've never developed a taste for it it's my own fault. Many years ago, while on holiday in France, I found lurking in a dark corner of a supermarket in a town called Sourdeval some battered tins of *bouillabaisse*. Tinned *bouillabaisse!* What a find! Never mind that this was in Normandy, far from the Mediterranean: back they came to Scotland in triumph, to be served to Francophile guests worthy of this honour. We tried a tin beforehand, just to ensure a private recapture of the Mediterranean sun, the sparkling sea, the wavelets lapping the toe-scorching sands, the scanty to non-existent etc., etc. . . .

. . . there was only one word for it: 'Gadz!' as children in the North-east of Scotland used to say when faced with something unusually revolting. We didn't get beyond a second spoonful, and even Bellamy refused the horrid mess, however heavily laced with Pedigree Chum. I hope it found its eventual way back to the sea. We would have done better with an American *bouillabaisse* recipe quoted sardonically by Alan Davidson, Grand Master of seafood writers, in his *Mediterranean Seafood*: "Put one can tomato soup and one can pea soup in top of double boiler and heat.' The recipe contains no fish, no herbs and no olive oil."

Time to go home. We whistle for Bellamy, who at last comes out of the water, shakes herself and jumps into the back of the car, dripping water that maybe once bore the hulls of Odysseus, St Paul, Richard Cœur de Lion or Horatio Nelson, not to mention Phoenician shellfish hunters. And M. Maigre's fish suppliers, to be sure.

Poetic Licence

Fernand Bonnery, a tenor in the St Pons choir and a man without guile, once asked me if I'd known Sir Sean Connery when I lived in Scotland, and I was sorry to have to say no, I'd never met him. Respectful, envious even, of Fernand's innocence before the fact that *connerie* is a far from polite word in French, I asked him why he wanted to know. Ah, he said, he'd had a little idea: some time before he'd organised a great get-together, indeed a clan gathering, of the Bonnery tribe. Anyone of the name of Bonnery that he could locate, his own extended family and many others from all over France, all were invited to Riols, his native village, to celebrate *le bonneryisme*, the state of being a Bonnery. It had been such a success that he was planning another: could it be possible, he wondered, that the name Connery was a corruption, a clerical error, a typo, a pseudonym for the real Bonnery lying beneath? It would be wonderful to gather the great man into the fold.

I said I thought it was unlikely. Fernand swallowed his disappointment like a true Bonnery, and went on to ask if I could possibly translate a questionnaire he'd prepared into English: ever in search of more Bonnerys, he was wanting to start enquiries in the United States. So I took it home to Olargues and Josephine and I worked on it, full of admiration for the vision and energy that was driving Fernand to canvass several hundred million people. When we asked him how many copies he wanted, he answered oh, just one would be enough.

We'd forgotten that Fernand was a local councillor and therefore had access to the secretarial facilities, including the copying machine, in the *mairie*. What became of his initiative we never found out, but every Wednesday night when my choir, Le Chœur de Hauts Cantons, met to rehearse in the Riols *mairie* we were reminded of another project he busied himself with, another shepherding, penning and categorisation of people.

Entrusted with the Riols archives, Fernand had hand-lettered, in a striking copperplate, lists of every village council since well before the Revolution of 1789. There's village history here, from the distant days when the first citizen of Riols was styled *consul* rather than *maire*, down to the present. His framed and glazed lists hang round the rehearsal room, a chronicle of the administration of the commune's affairs through the thick and thin of French history: through the *ancien régime*, the Revolution, Napoleonic empire, monarchy, Republic, defeat, Nazi occupation and recovery, a memorial to stalwart aldermanry and dedicated public service. Local names, Lignon, Barthès, Tailhades, reappear with every change of régime, a common thread through the fabric of the ages. Fernand Bonnery himself appears, a councillor since the most recent local election. All is worthiness and honour: at least, until you go through to the loo at the far end of the room, where civic pride takes a bit of a tumble from a printed notice reading (in translation): Gentlemen, you flatter yourselves. Please stand nearer the bowl.

* * *

Over the hills and into the Minervois, a region north of Narbonne and Carcassonne that gives its name to a range of wines chiefly remarkable for their diversity and unpredictability. We arrive in a village called Caunes Minervois, where we succumb yet again to one the great pleasures of living in the south of France, stopping for coffee at a *terrasse*, a pavement café. There's a fountain nearby, where water pipes embedded in an obelisk spurt feebly into a *bassin*. There are inscriptions on all four faces of the obelisk, mostly reminding us of the here-today-gone-tomorrow nature of our life, but the most unusual is almost a historical document:

> *Cette onde qui jaillit*
> *Et si pure et si belle*
> *Nous promet de nombreux*
> *Mais inconstants bienfaits*
> *Le temps peut la tarir*
> *Moins périssable qu'elle*
> *La bonté de nos rois*
> *Ne tarira jamais*

> This wave which gushes forth
> Both so pure and so fine
> Promises us numerous but unreliable benefits.
> In time it will dry up.
> Less perishable, the generosity of our kings
> Will never cease flowing.

You don't expect to come across publicly such abject monarchism in a land which sent Louis XVI to the guillotine, and you wonder which kings the inscription refers to. First thoughts might lead you to Louis XIV, the Sun King, a man of unquestionable generosity towards himself but not best known for forking out for public fountains in remote Languedoc villages. Look closer and there's not only a date, 1825, but the name of the king then reigning, Charles X, one of those inglorious French kings who slotted awkwardly into the period, sometimes called the July Monarchy, between the downfall of Napoleon after Waterloo and his nephew Louis Napoleon's coming to power in 1848.

Charles X is now plunged in the deepest oblivion, but time hasn't quite dried up the fountain. Whoever called the feeble, intermittent spurt *une onde*, a wave, had clearly binged on poetic licence. Or maybe he came from Riols?

FURTHER AFIELD

Collioure

It's only a few minutes from the Spanish border, but it doesn't strike you as a frontier village. In fact, it reinforces its Frenchness, gives itself a last shot of pure Gallicism before the language, colour, scenery and ambiance changes a couple of Mediterranean headlands further south. This is Collioure, and I expect the guide books refer to it as The Pearl of the Vermilion Coast, although they ought perhaps to describe it as the ruby or the sapphire, as the colours are mostly vivid reds and blues.

It's a gem in anyone's book, certainly in ours. We come back often, although mainly out-of-season to avoid the crowds drawn in summer to the seriously picturesque twin-harboured little fishing port cradled in a steep-to bay where the final eastern flourish of the Pyrenees, a range of pointed, castle-crowned peaks called Les Albères, plunges into the Mediterranean and creates a coastline of scalloped headlands and bays that become, further south, the Spanish Costa Brava, the Wild Coast. It looks as if Collioure has been washed ashore, and that what you're seeing from the corniche road above is Mediterranean flotsam and jetsam that has taken root and has grown into the delectable little port you wish you were the first to discover. And keep it a secret.

The secret's out now, though. Villas and apartments stretch up and over the hills enfolding the port like a bad case of chicken pox. You can't really grumble about the pedigree of the people who let the cat out of the bag: Matisse, Derain, Braque and others, who came again and again to Collioure to explore the gorgeous interplay of sunlight with sea, ochre roofs, colour-washed and balconied walls, fishing boats with triangular lateen sails, nets of glistening anchovies and the famous stone-built lighthouse at the old port entrance, now the church bell-tower, with its resident seagull perched on the rose-pink dome. There's a painting trail you can follow, with reproductions at the points where the artists set up their easels.

Picasso, too, is supposed to have come to Collioure, although I can't find chapter and verse for it. He was too people-oriented for the seriously picturesque to mean very much to him, although he would have been quick to see, with those mesmeric dark eyes of his, the strange anomaly posed by the three Collioure military establishments: Fort Miramar guarding the village to the north, Fort St Elme to the south, and on the promontory between the two harbours the Château Royal, brooding but impressive – and operational: as we walked along the seashore beneath its massive ramparts, a squad of naval commandos roared off in an inflatable and disappeared round the headland. *Si pacem vis, bellum para*, as the Roman strategist Vegetius wrote. If you want peace, prepare for war.

Here, enough of this long-haired stuff, as an American friend says when I start cracking on like this. Let's move on, fast. From *bellum* to belly, in fact. Much more interesting.

* * *

We ate at Le San Vicen, comfortably warm in winter sunshine, under the still leafless plane trees a few metres back from the water's edge. I don't think there's much point in going somewhere special if you

156

don't crystallise the experience with a meal, preferably a long, lingering lunch. San Vicen is Saint Vincent – a rocky islet just beyond the harbour, round which the commandos roared – in Catalan, and the Catalan influence is strong, in language as in cuisine. Also crystallising the experience that day was Michael Winner, film producer and food writer, perhaps the only man ever to wear a blazer at Collioure.

Was he eating the celebrated Collioure anchovies too? We were hidden from each other's view by one of the famous plane trees that shade the myriad summer tourists, so I can't tell you. Maybe like Josephine and me he moved on to the Catalan-inspired *calamars à la plancha*, seared slices of young squid. Mmm, *délicieux*.

At home the next day we were surprised to find a French television crew had been in Collioure to record an item about sunny spots in winter for the 1 o'clock news. It was all there, the sparkling sea, the bell tower, the brightly-painted boats drawn up on the beach, the *terrasse* of Le San Vicen, the waiter who served us, even two little girls who'd dared the water, which was more than we did. No blazered Michael Winner, though. He might have been behind the scenes directing the film crew, of course.

* * *

In the course of a happy weekend savouring Catalan seafood, we came across *garouinas*. *Oursins* in French, they're sea urchins, the spiky fellows that lurk on submerged rocks and send you running for the nearest beach gear shop for your jellies or flip-flops. Alan Davidson, the Grand Master of seafood writers, tells the unappealing story of a Frenchman who trod on one and was still removing fragments of spike as they emerged from his foot twelve years later.

Garouinas, fresh from the sea and uncooked, appear halved in a big dish with a tiny spoon, like a mustard spoon. On the underside of each urchin, which you handle as carefully as you would a chestnut husk, there are five small coral-pink ridges which you scrape off with your spoon and dab on a piece of bread, maybe with a dash of lemon. There isn't much to them: you need at least a dozen to give you a sense of having eaten anything at all. But the taste is the very essence of seaside: sun, breeze, spray, salt, ozone, the tang of seaweed and brine-washed shingle. Only oysters have the edge.

But just think. Somewhere, sometime in the recesses of time some beachcomber must have wrenched one of these things off its rock, smashed it open, scraped off the little pink ridges – the ovaries, in fact – with a salty fingernail and capered off home to his cave with the good news. I'm sure I'm not the first to remark that no matter how unusual or grotesque the life-form, someone, somewhere will have devised a means of eating it.

Albi

There's a deceptively comfortable feel to Albi. The outskirts of the city are all ring roads and light industry, housing estates and commercial centres heaving with new-look national chains like Decathlon (sports goods), Conforama, But and Fly (all budget furniture), but the centre is pink and pleasing. A short walk from the city centre car-park beneath the Place du Vigan, through traffic-free streets lined with smart boutiques selling mostly designer underwear, brings you to the heart of the city, built on an eminence beside the river Tarn.

The heart of Albi is dominated by the cathedral. There's little natural building stone in the area, so the older buildings are constructed of brick. This gives a mellow and comfortable feeling to the ancient centre of Albi, and a unique character to the mighty cathedral, a giant symbol of Catholic power and domination, which must have seemed alarmingly futuristic to the 13th-century Albigeois watching it rise brick by brick. It's a building unlike any other in the world, as far as I know. Apart from the ornate entrance porch, which was added later, the outside is mostly uniform and featureless. You look in vain for the virtuoso architectural ornament and tracery you normally associate with medieval cathedral building. If you didn't already know it was a cathedral, you wouldn't immediately assume it was a place of worship. It doesn't proclaim the soaring, flamboyant faith of its founders. It's difficult to know what to liken it to. A barracks? A prison? A fortress? A grain silo, even?

There's an uncomfortable reason for this. It's a power building, the ecclesiastical equivalent of William the Conqueror's Tower of London or Sir Edwin Lutyens' Parliament building in New Delhi, designed to assert the authority of the builder and cow the subjugated. In the case of Albi the subjugated were the Cathars, a legendary non-Catholic sect who had spread over the Languedoc. Even today, 800 years down the line, people in search of fresh, uncomplicated beliefs find Catharism compelling. The word Cathar means pure.

They believed in two worlds, each constantly striving to dominate the other. Night and day, good and evil, God and the Devil, body and soul. Body and soul, that's the clue. The things of the body lurked in the shadows, those of the soul basked in the sun. Satan ruled the material, physical world. Sex and marriage – and baptism – were condemned. (I remember talking to our erstwhile neighbour Jean-Claude, the doctor from Narbonne, about this. He thought vestiges of Catharism maybe still existed in its final heartlands, the lonely hills of the Corbières, where proportion of one-child families was greater than anywhere else in France.) Meat, milk, eggs and other animal products were discouraged. Jesus was an outstandingly enlightened teacher but wasn't divine. Priests had no monopoly of anything. Ideas like hell and purgatory were false. Sacraments like communion were meaningless. Only one sacrament had any significance, a sort of baptism of the soul, the *consolamentum*, just before death, releasing it to the realms of light. This was simply the touch of a *parfait* or *parfaite* (the word really means finished or complete), a Cathar man or woman whose life was recognised as being particularly pure.

Such heresy stuck in Rome's throat. The Cathar organisation, based on the four bishoprics of Albi, Toulouse, Carcassonne and Agen, was strong enough to resist persuasion, but in 1204, when Pope Innocent III's legate was murdered in the domain of Count Raymond VI of Toulouse, a crusade against the Cathar heretics was ordered. Innocent III called on the French king, Philippe-Auguste, to raise troops. The French king saw an unrepeatable chance of laying his hands on the hitherto independent Languedoc and the routes into Spain it lay astride. Conduct of the crusade was eventually entrusted to a well-connected thug called Simon de Montfort.

It took 40 years to reduce the Cathars. The last of many strongholds to fall was Montségur, an extraordinary hill-top fortress in the foothills of the Pyrenees. After a six-month siege the governor surrendered, against safe-conducts for his garrison: the truce did not cover the 207 Cathar refugees within his walls, among them his own wife and mother. Rather than renounce their faith, they marched of their own accord down from the castle to the flames below on the morning of March 16th, 1244, led by their bishop, Bertrand Marty. Much later somebody put up a memorial to them inscribed in Occitan:

ALS CATARS
ALS MARTIRS
DEL PUR AMOR
CRESTIAN

(To the Cathars, to the martyrs for pure Christian love)

By 1321, when Guillaume Bélibaste, the last Cathar *parfait*, had been burnt at the stake in Villerouge-Termenès in the remote fastnesses of the Corbières, the walls of the new Albi cathedral had risen, a mighty symbol of Catholic power and a stark reminder of the futility of challenging orthodox theology.

Fortress it may appear from the outside, but inside there's all the familiar paraphernalia of a large Catholic church, the decoration, the colour, the sculpted saints, the pin-drop acoustics. You wander about, dwarfed by the vastness, thinking your own private thoughts about all this until Wham! (or Paf! as the French say) – you're faced with the great medieval painted screen, separating the chapel of Sainte Cécile from the main choir, a kind of sanctuary behind the altar.

The Last Judgement is in full swing, although in 1693 some gormless dolt cut away the central figure of Christ the redeemer to make a doorway. In our hubristic 21st century way we might think it quaint, but the late medieval painters made certain it wasn't a pretty sight. The Book of Life records all our misdeeds. As usual, it's all right for the great and good, who find their way to heaven, but for us sinners there are six panels, representing the Seven Deadly Sins. There's one missing. It's never Lust, surely, the one Deadly Sin everyone has heard of? But no, here are the Lustful, bare-breasted and priapic *in extremis*, tumbling through space to the everlasting flames licking at their loins. My mind strays to Gilbert and Sullivan's Mikado: 'My object all sublime, I shall achieve in time – to let the punishment fit the crime, the punishment fit the crime.' The Gluttonous, so obese that they can hardly bear their own weight, hurtle through the void to the cauldrons below to be rendered down into yet more fat. So with the Envious, the Avaricious, the Angry and the Proud. The Idle are strangely absent. Did medieval theologians excuse Idleness? Or perhaps they just couldn't be bothered to turn up for the Last Judgement? But no, it's neither. What fate was reserved for the Idle we shall have to make an effort to imagine, because their punishment was cut away, with the figure of Christ above, to make the doorway.

Indeed, the man- and woman-kind condemned to eternal punishment are depicted as a sorry lot, lame, deformed, disfigured, one-legged, scarred, scabrous, life's walking wounded . . . we'd better move on.

Next door to the cathedral is the rather earlier Berbie palace, 'Berbie' apparently being a corruption of the Occitan word 'bisbia', meaning bishop, but I'm suspicious of over-glib etymologies like this. However, much of this very fine building is devoted to a Toulouse-Lautrec museum, and here are the originals of those famous posters of Aristide Bruant, La Goulue, Jane Avril, Valentin le Désossé ('the boneless') and other once bright but now ghostly lights of the Paris cabaret *demi-monde* who so fascinated Toulouse-Lautrec.

Toulouse-Lautrec, scion of a noble house who suffered childhood accidents which virtually deprived him of the use of his legs, had a house in a village called Boussagues, in the Hérault *département*, many kilometres to the south-east of Albi. From Boussagues it was a short ride to Lamalou les Bains, a place with thermal mud springs reputed to be effective in treating, among other conditions, venereal diseases. Who first made this discovery, and how, I leave others to ponder. Nor do I know how effective Toulouse-Lautrec found the treatment. In the later years of the 19th century a casino was built there, for the entertainment of wealthy sufferers while they underwent the cure. The casino is still working, although the gaming machines give way to a season of light opera – not, so far, *The Mikado* – in summer. Nowadays the village is the southern French centre for physiotherapy. There's a curious notion that the Italian mafia sends its wounded to Lamalou for treatment, so that when you see a man with his arm in plaster feeding a casino fruit machine you're not certain which is the one-armed bandit.

The clinics operate all the year round and by all accounts provide a marvellous service. Cynics wonder sometimes if patient numbers aren't artificially kept up by the profusion of cracked and uneven pavement slabs and low-level traffic bollards, a constant hazard to the many wheelchairs you see up and down the street. But you're safe enough on the *terrasse* of the the PMU café, the very civilised French equivalent of the UK betting shop. I'm afraid we're not that interested in the turf, but their coffee is excellent. Having bought a paper from the Maison de la Presse across the road, we settle down to read the news from home and idly watch the passers-by, the lame, the deformed, the disfigured, the one-legged, the scarred, the scabrous, life's walking wounded . . . but this is where we came in, isn't it?

We stayed overnight in Albi once a day or two before *la fête des pères*, the mid-June Fathers' Day in France. Josephine discovered a Geneviève Lethu shop on the cathedral square. Geneviève Lethu is a national franchise for up-market-ish small domestic goods, a sort of French Habitat with the corners rubbed off. She came out with a gift-wrapped package, which she presented to me as an early Fathers' Day present. Agog, I opened it when we sat down on the *terrasse* of the Le Grand Pontié, a large café on the Place du Vigan, for a pre-dinner drink.

It turned out to be a pepper mill, just the very thing that every father has always wanted for Father's Day. True, our old one had worn out – to quote from the Old Testament book Ecclesiastes (Chapter 12 Verse 3, if you want to check) 'the grinders cease because they are few' – and needed replacing. What struck me as remarkable was the maker's name: Peugeot, and no, it wasn't a promotional gimmick from the car manufacturers.

Josephine had the story. It's a kind of dualism all over again, a duality of belief matching that of the Cathars, each world trying to dominate the other. In 1806 the Peugeots of Montbéliard, almost on the Swiss frontier, started a factory making metal goods. 80 years or so later two brothers inherited the family works. One tinkered about trying to produce a self-propelled vehicle. The other, disdaining his brother's conviction that there was any future in horseless carriages, saw a rosier future in kitchenware. As far as I know the Book of Life doesn't record what the Peugeot brothers' children felt about their various inheritances.

I associate it in my mind with President Mitterand, but maybe it goes back beyond him to the days of his predecessor, Giscard d'Estaing: it's the principle known as *désenclavement,* the opening up of remote country. It was expressed in human terms as the notion that no settlement in mainland France should be more than 15 minutes' drive from a major road.

For most of the country the idea was at least feasible, but the nettle to be grasped was the *massif central,* the roof of France, the huge upland and often mountainous region in southern and central France, where life is about as easy as in the Scottish Highlands: the climate is what the French call *rude,* sheep probably outnumber human beings by at least 2 to 1, and some of the *départements* in the *massif central* – Cantal, Aveyron, Lozère – are among the least populated and least known in France. To open up the *massif central* meant driving a motorway south from Clermont Ferrand, taking it up to 1000 metres and more for much of its length and bringing it down again sharply to the Languedoc plains to finish up in the Mediterranean sun at Béziers.

French motorways are generally privately run, but this one, the A75 and subtitled La Méridionale, was financed by the government in a commendable display of an administration putting its money where its mouth was. The project was started in the late 1980s, and slowly the tarmac ribbon sculpted its graceful course up and down valleys, over rolling moorland and sheep-dotted hill pasture, round the shoulders of volcanic outcrops, across arid stretches of limestone *causse,* bending sinuously like a slow-motion wing three-quarter past forests and windswept, tiny-windowed farmhouses, making the road a semi-divine joy to drive, justifying to the last penny everything you'd forked out for a driveworthy car until you came to the town of Millau.

Millau (pronounced Mee-yoh), lying on the upper reaches of the river Tarn, is a medium-sized town known for gloves and – until the bridge was opened – cursing motorists. Giant, impassable limestone cliffs between canyons dominate the town to the east and south, but to the west the river has carved itself a steeply-sided valley about a mile wide. How to take the new motorway across this valley, and relieve one of the worst bottlenecks in France?

The question was put to commercial tender, and a firm called Eiffage came up with the idea of a super-bridge, winning the contract with a breathtaking design by Sir Norman Foster. After two or three years in the building the bridge was finally opened by the President, and, to cut this story as short as the route from Clermont Ferrand to Béziers has now become, we went to see the new bridge in all its bandbox freshness a week or two after the opening ceremony. We mentioned where we were going to François the *maçon* and his sidekick Frédérique, Frédo for short – very suitably as he's not the tallest man you've ever seen, although he plays up front for Olargues FC – who were laying flagstones that day on one of our terraces. They came up with an unusual story we'd somehow missed out on.

The new bridge was opened to ordinary traffic 48 hours after the President cut the tape, they said, and as usual there was some competition to be the first member of the public to drive across. The honours went to somebody who'd parked at an advantageous point on the approaches several days before. So over he went ahead of everyone else and got his name in the local papers and was featured in that evening's regional television news programme and no doubt the pleasure he took from his primacy had its origins in a fatal obsession he had with the bridge. 'Over he went' maybe isn't the most sensitive term to use, because the day before our little outing the very same man drove to the centre of the bridge, stopped his car, got out, climbed over the side-screens and threw himself into the void.

Any unease this sad tale might have caused was masked by our first view of the bridge. Approaching from the south, you come on it suddenly, like a tall ship, a gigantic seven-masted schooner hanging in the air. We'd seen pictures of it under construction, and our immediate thought was oh goodness, vertigo: we'll never make it across without

1. Being sick, or
2. Passing out, or
3. Being seized by an irresistible urge to drive over the side.

It wasn't anything like that at all, of course. As with any bridge, you're conscious of the distant view, and indeed there's a panoramic view of ochre-tiled Millau a kilometre or two upstream and the cliffs and bluffs beyond the town. But the designers have fitted incurving wind screens to the edges of the bridge, and if you hadn't been told that you were riding at a dizzy 270 metres (about 880 feet) above the surface of the river Tarn, making it the world's highest/longest road bridge, you wouldn't know anything about it.

It's soon over. Less than a minute to glide past the seven great white pylons and their serried stays, planing slightly downwards and to the right. Once you've reached the other side, the road sweeps gracefully back to the left, tracing what William Hogarth called the Line of Beauty. Is this deliberate? Who knows?

We drove on, stopping to pay our dues at the tollbooth a little further on (the bridge is the only part of the A75 that attracts a toll, the rest is free) and then breaking our journey at l'Aire de l'Aveyron, a bright, clean and well-equipped service station just outside Sévérac le Château, which sells just about everything you could possibly want except postcards of the famous bridge.

People were always asking for postcards, the girl behind the counter said. She was sorry, she didn't have any: the builders had the exclusive right to produce and sell postcards of their bridge. They were only available at the bridge visitor centre, at ground level between the bridge and Millau. H'm. So we drove back again, feeling that we'd made an infinitesimally tiny investment in this marvellous piece of engineering in simply driving across it, postcard or no postcard to prove it.

* * *

We have five bridges in Olargues. Two are utilitarian road bridges, linking the village with the main road the other side of the river Jaur, one is a railway bridge designed by Gustav Eiffel (the first four letters of whose surname survive in the civil enginering company responsible for the Millau bridge), the fourth carries a minor road over a railway cutting, and the fifth . . . well now, there's a curious thing.

The fifth Olargues bridge is the Pont du Diable, the Devil's Bridge, a narrow, hump-backed stone-built bridge dating from the 12th century. Devil's Bridges abound all over Europe for some reason. Maybe in the popular imagination the diabolically clever feat of making a wide-span stone arch stand up and bear weight linked the engineer with the Devil, maybe such hermetic know-how could only be obtained through a satanic pact. In Olargues – and elsewhere – the legend runs that the mediaeval bridge had to be completed by a certain deadline. For reasons best known to himself the Devil had no wish to see the bridge completed, and during the night demolished what had been built during the day, hurling the stones into the Jaur many feet below. Despairing of completion by the due date, the villagers sent their priest to negotiate with the Devil. The Devil's terms were harsh: he would allow the bridge to be finished on condition that the first living creature to cross the new bridge should be his. The priest returned, heavy-hearted, and the villagers took counsel. On the day of completion the villagers advanced *en masse* to the apex of the bridge, where the Devil waited for his due. Suddenly the ranks parted and a villager tossed a cat ahead of everyone else – and we've read elsewhere about the Olargues cats – and into the Devil's arms as his tribute. Outwitted, the Devil snarled diabolical curses and disappeared in the traditional puff of green smoke.

167

What is it with bridges and propitiation? What primeval instinct is there to ensure the passage with some kind of sacrificial offering? The Latin word for a priest, one who sought the favour of the gods with sacrifices on behalf of the his people, was 'pontifex', literally one who builds bridges. There's something very strange going on here.

Sand and snow

A birthday trip one snowy February took us to the Basque country, a green and hilly land at the Atlantic end of the Pyrenees, in the crook of the Bay of Biscay. Like Catalan, the language that straddles the Pyrenees at the eastern end, the Basque language knows no frontier and is spoken on both sides of the river Bidassoa, which forms the Franco-Spanish border.

To linguists Basque is utterly intractable. In vain can you search for the slightest resemblance to any other language in the world. Woe betide any monoglot Brit trying to make himself understood in southern Europe simply by sticking an O on the end of English words: 'More-o beer-o, over here-o' might work in the fleshpots of the Costa del Sol, but not in the Basque country. It's a one-off, the oldest surviving European language, a relic of a very ancient people resisting disappearance like a persistent patch of snow in a sheltered mountain gully.

The linguistic souvenirs we took home from a day or two in the region of St Jean de Luz, a fishing port and seaside resort just south of Biarritz which might have been quite pretty if we'd been able to see it through the driving snow, were meagre: *honda*, meaning sand, *ez horregatik*, no problem, and *eskerrik asco*, meaning thank you very much. Not what you might call a working vocabulary, the circumstances in which you might need to say 'Sand, no problem, thank you very much' being fairly limited.

168

And yet . . . in the late summer of 1813 British, German, Portuguese and Spanish troops under the command of the Duke of Wellington had virtually chased Napoleon's armies out of Spain. By September of that year Marshal Soult stood firm in a series of fortified positions behind the river Bidassoa, daring Wellington to set foot on French soil. The bridges had been destroyed, the Pyrenean passes upstream of the Bidassoa had been garrisoned and fortified. The river seemed impregnable and France seemed inviolable, especially as Wellington, having deployed troops up and down the Spanish bank of the river, did nothing.

Or so it seemed. In fact Wellington's intelligence, fine-tuned by a remarkable man known to the British as Colonel Colquhoun Grant and to the Spaniards as Granto el Bueno (maybe there is something to adding a final O after all) had discovered something that Soult wasn't aware of. On the southern, Spanish, side of the Bidassoa estuary, maybe 300 metres across the water from the French town of Hendaye, lies Fuenterrabia, a walled town with an ancient castle, refurbished some 300 years earlier by the Emperor Charles V. (It's now a magnificent *parador*, a Spanish Ministry of Tourism hotel.) The Basques, however, call this place Hondaribbia. We know what 'honda' means, and maybe Wellington's intelligence officers guessed that 'ribbia' meant ford. If the Bidassoa estuary was fordable, the French defences could be turned, and at little cost, given the few troops Soult had assigned to defending Hendaye. Local fishermen confirmed that at very low tides the estuary was fordable: there were at least two places where the exposed sandbanks gave a firm enough footing to cross. Aha. Could the following dialogue possibly have taken place?

British intelligence officer: *Honda?*
Basque fisherman: *Ez horregatik!*
British intelligence officer: *Eskerrik asco.*

We went to Hondarribia under leaden skies, heavy with snow –

very suitably, we wore wellington boots — to stroll along the broad promenade beneath the castle ramparts, looking at the river while waiting for an appointment to have my hair cut. The tide was on the turn, a little ferry crossed from Hondaribbia to Hendaye opposite following a curious dog-leg course, and as the tide went out banks of sand and shingle appeared. So, *plus ça change* . . .

Wellington had to wait until October 7th for a low enough tide to allow his troops to cross. William Napier, the great historian of the Peninsular War, who was present, wrote:

> The night set in heavily. A sullen thunder-storm... towards morning rolling over the Bidassoa fell in its greatest violence upon the French positions. During this turmoil Wellington...disposed a number of guns and howitzers along the crest of San Marcial, and his columns attained their respective positions along the banks of the river.
>
> As all the tents were left standing in the camps of the allies, the enemy could perceive no change on the morning of the 7th, but at seven o'clock, the fifth division and lord Aylmer's brigade emerging from their concealment took the sands in two columns... No shot was fired, but when they had passed the fords of the low-water channel a rocket was sent up from the steeple of Fuenterrabia as a signal. Then the guns and howitzers opened from San Marcial, the troops made for the Jonco ford, and the passage above the bridge also commenced. From the crest of San Marcial seven columns could be seen...those above the bridge plunging at once into the fiery contest, those below it appearing in the distance like huge sullen snakes winding over the heavy sands.
>
> ...the French, completely surprised, permitted even the brigades of the fifth division to gain the right bank and form their lines, before a hostile musket flashed.

In all some 24 000 troops crossed the Bidassoa that day, and the nation that had invaded so many others under Napoleon over the previous fifteen years found itself invaded. Wellington's progress continued until Easter 1814, by which time he had reached Toulouse, Napoleon had abdicated and the war was over, at least until it flared up again with the Waterloo campaign the following year.

Wellington's men were mostly too young to have known France before the Revolution. They found a delectable land whose countryfolk were eager to place themselves under British protection, safe from the exactions of Soult's retreating armies. British forces were strictly forbidden to pillage or help themselves to anything. Fearing that his Spanish troops would loot as they had in earlier years been looted by the French, Wellington sent them home once the Bidassoa had been crossed. It was a popular move, and the British found themselves unexpectedly welcome. Some stayed: many were attracted to Pau, in the foothills of the Pyrenees. The Pau hunt was apparently a relic of Wellington's cavalrymen. I believe they even played cricket there at one time.

Now I come to think of it we learnt another Basque word. In a Hondaribbia restaurant we stamped the snow off our boots, settled ourselves and asked the raven-haired, dark-eyed, black-clad and very attentive waitress her name. Ehurre, she said, it's the Basque for snow. Absolutely. *Ez horregatik.*

Gone for Launch

My first thoughts on arriving at the hotel Bleu Marine in St Raphaël weren't very charitable. There was such an incredible noise, like a surreal fairground or railway station music: you couldn't separate out the strands of music because of the booming echo and the overlay of other sounds, traffic, children playing, doors opening and closing down the corridor, people laughing round the bar downstairs. *If that flaming disco doesn't stop there'll be trouble* . . .

Josephine, as always much calmer and more collected, said she was sure it would and stepped out on to the balcony with a view over the Bleu Marine swimming pool, into which a couple of presumably untenanted plastic poolside loungers had been gusted, to the crowded and bobbing marina beyond and the white horses of the Mediterranean stretching to the horizon. The noise screamed and howled in fifty different sharps and flats. It wasn't a disco at all, of course: it was the *mistral*, which blows for days on end, the Provençal north wind with the ice of the Alps in its teeth, had found a thousand masts and ten thousand taut forestays and halyards to thrum and drone in a demonic, unnerving wail.

Not a good augury for the Great Launch the next day. Clint and Annabel (not their real names: I asked them what they really wanted to be called when they were children and they came up with this. H'm.) were pushing the boat out, literally and metaphorically. This was Chapter 1 of A Life On The Ocean Wave, golden years of retirement to be spent cruising the Mediterranean, from St Raphaël to Marbella, from Ibiza to Capri, to Corfu, maybe finally, like returning Odysseus, to Ithaca. It was clearly the occasion for a champagne launch.

But foaming champagne and a howling *mistral* aren't good bedfellows. The *Dawn Treader* (again, not her real name, nor any reference to Clint's and Annabel's homecoming habits from waterfront night-clubs) was far too new and pristine to have a bottle of Mumm or Veuve Cliquot cracked over her bows. In any case she was already in the water, swaying at her berth as the cockpit filled with guests. Such a waste of champagne, too . . . but King Neptune, lord of the wind and waves, claimed his tribute all the same.

The great art of opening champagne, unless you've just won the Ashes or the Formula 1 championship, is to keep the bottle still and ease the cork out so gently that there's the merest whisper of escaping bubbles or, as some have put it, with just the sigh of a contented woman. No such *finesse*, however, from my cockpit neighbour, the French agent who'd sold Clint and Annabel the *Dawn Treader* and who was obviously a supporter of the Big Bang theory when it came to loosening the cork. The *mistral* snatched at the foaming cascade from the shaken bottle, flung it in a bubbling spatter across the water and over the deck and sprayed it all over his wife's windcheater.

She barely noticed, pausing only to flick an errant droplet out of her eye. Her windcheater, like her husband's, was a very pale greeny-yellow and didn't show the stains. We imagined them earlier that morning wondering what to wear. Champagne launches must be all in a day's work to them, getting sprayed an occupational hazard: they must put on champagne-stain resistant clothing as readily as you and I would find an old pair of gloves to prune the roses in.

Decisions about what to wear may have troubled another of the St Raphaël waterfront residents, no connection with the launch, but an elderly *grande dame* of the utmost *chic* on her way with her impeccably groomed West Highland white terrier to collect her daily *baguette*. Jeans, old sweater, flip-flops, the usual quayside kit? No, no. Court shoes, rings and bracelets and . . . a full length mink coat. Just as well that the Big Bang theorist was otherwise occupied when she passed.

The *mistral* died down the next day and a maiden voyage was possible. The *Dawn Treader* slipped out of her berth under a cloudless sky with Captain Clint at the wheel, her diesel engine purring as only a split-new Volvo Penta can, along the marina fairway and then out beyond the harbour wall, and into open sea, an equally split-new Red Duster flapping proudly from the backstay.

This flag was a present from some other guests at the launch, a quartet of Charlton Athletic supporters, among the more unexpected phenomena that weekend at St Raphaël. The Big Bang theorist asserted that the Red Duster was illegal, at least flown at the stern: how could a craft registered in Toulon – and indeed the letters TL were obvious on the stern – fly anything but the French *tricolor*?

Captain Clint was unrepentant. He'd change it in a day or two, but for the moment he was going to leave it there out of respect for the Charlton Athletic fans, to whom he'd accorded the honour of crewing for the maiden voyage. He was feeling bullish, the Nelson Touch was upon him. Did we know what Napoleon had said to Admiral Villeneuve on the eve of Trafalgar? To the water: it is the hour. *A l'eau: c'est l'heure.* You've got it, of course: Hallo, sailor. Ho ho ho.

We watched them from the quayside out of sight, listening intently in case the ship's company should suddenly break into song (well, we did have *Rule, Britannia!* the day before) and *One Shaun Bartlett, There's Only One Shaun Bartlett* should come wafting across the sun-sparkling waters like the song of the Sirens in the *Odyssey*. (For the uninitiated, Shaun Bartlett plays, or played, up front for Charlton Athletic.) If they did, they were too far out on a course for St Tropez for us to hear them. Too bad. You can't have everything, can you?

HEART OF THE LANGUEDOC

A Priori

Who was the mysterious benefactor who first endowed the Prieuré?
What led Marshal Soult to donate a stolen bell?
What do women want most in the world?
Will Eric's anti-English club take off?
Will we live here in the Languedoc for ever?

* * *

There's a tidy little mystery here, one that far outclasses the infantile bletherings of the Da Vinci code or the Rennes le Château puzzle, which isn't a mystery at all but a hilarious exercise in gullibility. Why has the little man got his hand over his mouth?

Let me explain. We're at the Prieuré de St Julien, a place of great tranquillity and ease of the spirit. If ever you longed for peace on earth, you will find it here, although true peace lies in the heart and mind of man and not in his creations. If ever you found yourself stumbling under the weight of life's problems, you can slip them off and stretch your aching limbs and back for a moment or two. If ever you wanted to feel at one with all those people over many centuries who have drawn fresh breath and seen new horizons, you can sense their benign presence here. This is a very special place.

* * *

Over a long period in the remote past the river Jaur, loveliest and least-known of the rivers of the deep South, carved itself a valley, a weathered cleft between the dragon-toothed mountains of the Espinouse and the softer, more rounded hills of the Avant Monts, the last hills before the Languedoc plain and the Mediterranean. Here and there in this geologically very varied area the river met obstacles of harder rock, which it and its tributaries by-passed, leaving lumps and spurs scattered along the floor and sides of the valley. Olargues is built on one such lump, and three or four kilometres away the church builders, at about the time of Charlemagne or Alfred the Great, put up a little chapel on a sunny promontory dominating the valley below. It was dedicated to St Julian. This doesn't point us in any particular direction: there are at least 32 Julians in the Catholic calendar of saints.

Goodness knows whose wealth was lavished on this mini-masterpiece of Romanesque architecture. Somebody cared enough about it to finance the transport of a particular dark red sandstone, the colour of dried blood, from what is now the Corrèze *département*, many kilometres to the north. Such a 9th century journey implies ox-cart load after ox-cart load, groaning and heaving along primitive roads southwards from the quarries of Collonges la Rouge. It's a fearful journey, across rolling plateaux intersected by the gorges of the great rivers of southern France, Dordogne, Lot, Aveyron and Tarn, and when eventually you arrive at the southern edge of the Massif Central the tableland suddenly falls away in a jumble of crags and cliffs, spikes and narrow clefts – the Espinouse mountains, in fact – with very few convenient descents on foot, let alone by ox-cart. A penitential journey, horrific enough in the contemplation of it to make you think surely, surely this blood-red stone must have had a more local origin. But it's not the case.

The original chapel has a northern feel to it, in any case. If you have a mind for such things you wonder what it's doing in a remote spot in the Languedoc. There are similar churches in the Auvergne, many indeed dedicated to St Julian, where local grey or white stone has been decorated or highlighted with the same dark red sandstone. At the Prieuré de St Julien the door and window embrasures are faced with it, interior arches are lined with it, the decorative panel above the main door is composed of alternate lozenges of white and red, the outside walls – ah, here we are at last at this intriguing little mystery: on the outside wall, at the extreme eastern point of the apse, a significant place in any church because it's the nearest point to Jerusalem, there's a red sandstone corbel or boss carved into the shape of a man's head, but with his hand over his mouth. What secret is he guarding? What mustn't we know? What has he been sworn to secrecy over? Whatever it is, he can keep a long-term secret: he's been there since about 850AD.

The Prieuré kept its beautiful lines and proportions for 800 years, when the 17th century church authorities decided to enlarge it. They tore down the north wall and rebuilt it entirely in local stone two or three metres further out, leaving the apse untouched. In addition to changing the roof line, this had the curious effect of displacing the altar from the central axis. A large presbytery or hospice was built adjoining the chapel, probably on the site of an earlier one. At the same time a tower was built, with an outside stair and gallery for access to the belfry. A cockleshell was carved into the masonry of the gallery, and this gives a clue to one aspect of the Prieuré's functions and identities.

A cockleshell was – and is – the emblem of pilgrimage to Santiago de Compostella, in north-western Spain. Many ancient pilgrim routes pass through France, converging at the western end of the Pyrenees.

The most southerly route, and the least demanding, leads from Arles in Provence to Montpellier, thence to Clermont l'Hérault, Bédarieux and St Pons de Thomières before continuing to Toulouse. Visible on its promontory for kilometres around, the Prieuré de St Julien stands on this route, offering spiritual and physical refreshment and support to passing pilgrims. They would have recognised the prominent cockleshell, certainly, and would have felt instantly at home. They might also have given a firm identity to the dedicatee: one of the 32 St Julians, who is probably a composite of the virtues of several other Julians, is nicknamed The Hospitaller.

At the Revolution of 1789 the Whitefriars, who had run the Prieuré from the beginning, departed, and the chapel became the parish church serving the scattered settlements of Le Cros, Les Castagnès, Mauroul, Auziale and others, gathered together in a *commune* taking its name from the shadowy saint of the Prieuré. Today Mass is occasionally celebrated there, one of 48 other places of worship, served by 2 priests, in the local group of parishes. In summer, however, there are various religious activities led by small group of Dominican monks, cousins of the Augustinian Whitefriars, who come to stay in the presbytery for a few weeks. The company is sometimes quite distinguished: a Vatican theologian, promoted to cardinal shortly before the death of Pope Jean-Paul II, makes his summer retreat at the Prieuré.

* * *

For better or worse the Prieuré is most often used for concerts. There's a perfect acoustic, ideal for soloists and small groups. For a year or two, parallel with my duties as Titular Organist in nearby Olargues, I organised Prieuré concerts. The most arduous aspect of this was turning down musicians who had fallen in love with the place so deeply that they wanted to come back year after year. I went up once to prepare for a piano recital, driving up from the valley floor through the vineyards, olive groves, cherry orchards and stands of evergreen oak. One or two others were there: Eric, a sound engineer, busy with cables, stands and microphones, and Fr Grimaldi, one of the white-habited summer Dominicans, an interesting man, entirely approachable.

While we are talking the bell in the tower rings out 6 o'clock. It has a muffled sound, as though the bell is slightly cracked. Or maybe there's another explanation? The automatic striking mechanism is unstoppable, short of disconnecting the Prieuré's electricity supply, which means that it will chime during the concert. What's more, in the Midi fashion it rings the hours twice, in case you miss it the first time. Some musicians find this quaint, especially when its note harmonises with the music they're playing, but some of the regular audience find it distracting. Eric the recording engineer despairs. Jean-Claude, the president of the Concert Society, has often threatened to deal with it. Has he been up there in the belfry, trying to muffle it with a blanket or one of those sausage-shaped French bolsters?

Fr Grimaldi laughs. He doesn't think so. The bell has undergone many adventures, he tells me, but as far as he knows no one has succeeded in silencing it. It has 'Montserrat' embossed on it, he says, and I wonder if he too has climbed up there to see, Dominican robes flowing. It was *butin de guerre*, war booty, he says, ransacked from the great Catalan monastery of Montserrat by Napoleon's troops under Marshal Nicolas Jean-de-Dieu Soult, who gave the bell to the Prieuré. We've met him before: he was the man who left the back door ajar at Hondaribbia. I don't know what connection Marshal Soult ever had with the Prieuré, except that his family home was at St Amans, forty minutes or so to the west.

If he donated the bell to ring out for his victories, he would have had a long wait, I suggest to Fr Grimaldi, because he never won a battle in his life; at least not against the British in the Peninsula. Of course Napoleon left him the Duke of Wellington to contend with.

Fr Grimaldi looks surprised, as well he might. The French have a curious habit of glossing over battles they might not have won. (The British are no different: have you ever heard of Chillianwallah? No? Well, there you are, then. And even Dunkirk, which Churchill described as a colossal military disaster, has been legendized into some kind of mighty victory.) If you've been to the battlefield of Waterloo, where Soult was Napoleon's chief of staff, you'll understand. You wouldn't think any British had ever been there.

He died in his bed, at any rate, Fr Grimaldi says. No soldier could wish for more.

At 10 o'clock, halfway through the recital, the bell strikes the hour, twice as usual, and twenty muffled strokes resound above the barrage of mighty Lisztian chords the pianist is thundering out of the Steinway. Heady stuff. And pretty cacophonous. Perhaps at this point the little man in stone on the other side of the apse wall has his hands over his ears rather than over his mouth. Maybe his secret, or a tiny part of it, is that St Julian the Hospitaller is the patron saint of various groups of mankind, among them musicians and strolling minstrels.

* * *

Good heavens, here's a wedding going on. Clearly someone's trying to harness the magic of the Prieuré into their union. How wise. Let's go in. We're just in time: we're a few seconds ahead of the bride. There's a neat, trim woman wearing Finnish national costume on the door. Finnish? You never know what's coming next. She speaks to us in French, shows us to seats at the back. Standing in the aisle beside us are two trumpeters in evening dress, blowing softly into their instruments to keep them warm. We settle ourselves and look around. There must be eighty people here. No one is saying anything. They're waiting in complete silence.

We're captivated by the serenity of the place, bright and festal with flowers, arrangements of white roses, the inescapable gypsophylla, branches of bay and olive. There's a stark simplicity about it, an uncomplicatedness that speaks to the heart. A phrase of St Jerome come to mind: *sancta simplicitas*, holy simplicity. There's a calm, easeful beauty that needs no propping up, no justifying with statues or images.

Suddenly someone's mobile rings, and there's a laugh. The celebrant, a tall bearded man in a red shirt, reminds the assembly to switch their mobile phones off. In English. What have we come to? At this moment the Finnish lady tries to open both panels of the ancient double doors to admit the bride and her train. The doors are recalcitrant: it's only by giving a violent, unladylike kick to the less used panel that they both swing wide. More laughter. The trumpeters beside us sound a sparkling fanfare which sounds suspiciously like The Monkees' *I'm a believer*.

The veiled bride has her back to us as she processes down the off-centre aisle and takes station next to her waiting groom in front of the altar. Her meynie of tiny bridesmaids, like Moth, Cobweb, Peaseblossom and Mustardseed in *A Midsummer Night's Dream*, are dispersed to their parents in forward pews. A small choir, uniformed in red and black, stands up in horseshoe formation round the apse to sing a chorus from *The Marriage of Figaro* in Italian, accompanied by flute and piano. We're not certain what language it's all going to settle down into, and we begin to wonder whether it matters: maybe the important things in life transcend language. But we still haven't seen the bride from the front.

Things take a definitive plunge into English when the first reading is announced as *The Owl and the Pussy-Cat*, a set piece for the sort of humanist, non-liturgical wedding this is turning out to be, led by the tall celebrant in the red shirt, who tells us that the principals are man and wife already, having been married that morning in a civil ceremony in their local *mairie*. The second reading is delivered with aplomb and obvious enjoyment by an equally tall young man in full Moss Bros. morning dress: he gives us *Sir Gawain and the Lady Ragnell*, an Arthurian story, not one in the regular Round Table canon. It's a redemption legend, pregnant with deeper significances. It turns on Sir Gawain finding the right answer to the question of what women want most in the world, and the climax comes when the love and sacrifice of a good man releases a loathly hag from the thrall of an evil spell and transforms her into – what else? – a beautiful woman. This is justly popular with the Prieuré company, who give the reader a round of applause.

After the exchange of undertakings and rings and the lifting of her veil for a bridal kiss, she turns to face us, at last, and the company is invited to file up to salute the bride and groom. She is beautiful, as all women are on their wedding day, in an original 1950s mid-calf-length strapless oyster satin dress, embroidered at the bodice. We can feel the radiance from her, although we learn later on that this is as much due to the friction of *la bise* from the entire company, which includes many whiskered men, as from her own happiness. The trumpets sound again, bride and groom lead the procession out, and presently everyone swirls about a-bristle with cameras on the gravelled forecourt beneath the cockleshell and an immense horse chestnut tree, while on the hillside below the cherry trees are in white blossom and the vines are in April leaf.

People are beginning to relax. We overhear a middle-aged man engaged in a gentle flirtation with the flautist, or flautation with the flirtist, I don't mind: 'I'd give my right arm to play the flute like you.' We disappear before he starts on the old joke about the One-Armed Flautist.

* * *

Je vais monter une association anglophobe, I'm going to start up an anti-English society, Eric the sound engineer says to me before another Prieuré concert. It's nothing personal, don't be distressed, *mais les Anglais, c'est ras le bol,* I've had it up to here with the English. If it was personal, he says, delicacy would forbid me to mention it to you.

I'm very surprised. Eric is a good-hearted and sensitive man, the soul of consideration and kindness, although he has decided views on which musicians are worth recording and which don't justify a round trip of 300 kilometres from his home almost two *départements* away.

I ask him why he's got it in for the English and it all pours out. I'm expecting him to say *Je suis pas raciste, moi, mais . . .* (Me, I'm not racist, but . . .) and as usually happens when people come out with this, their very next words proclaim a pretty deep-seated prejudice. But I've done him an injustice: it's nothing to do with the English being English (by English he means British), although it's clear that their cleaving to certain vestigial colonial tendencies doesn't appeal to him. It's nothing to do with past rivalries, either.

He tells me about his village, a run-of-the-mill Midi settlement with close-clustered houses and a belt of small villas on the outskirts. Few village houses have gardens, some have courtyards, most have terraces or balconies at least. It's within easy reach of a provincial airport served by budget airlines. Every house, every decrepit old drum that comes on the market is snapped up by the English. They'll pay anything, Eric says, idiot prices. Estate agents and *notaires* rub their hands when they see them coming, especially if they don't speak French, and most don't. So do local builders.

Wouldn't you rather see these old village houses restored and lived in than left to rot and collapse? I ask.

No, I would not, Eric says. I'd rather see them pulled down and the village modernised. I wouldn't know, it's maybe an attractive idea across the Channel to own a holiday house, an old house in a traditional Midi village, as though it was a toy. What I do know is that we don't want to live in a museum. Or in a toyshop. But that's not my first complaint. The real trouble is that the English have pushed house prices up so far and so fast that they've priced the French out of the market. We can't live in our own country. It's an absolute scandal. They've done something about it in Chamonix, in the Alps. Maybe you've heard. They've put a quota on the number of houses that can be sold to foreigners, and put a cap on the price of apartments. Young people can afford to live there now. The sooner they do the same here the better.

In my village, Eric goes on, there used to be a post office, shops, a primary school, a doctor, *une terrasse*. (By *terrasse*, Eric means a bar or café where you can sit outside.) That's all gone, thanks to the English.

Most of them only come in the summer, so their houses stay shut up most of the year. There's less and less work, so people of working age and their children leave for the towns. The old people stay on for a bit until they die or go into old peoples' homes. There are only three French families left in my village. All the other houses are owned by the English. Maybe one or two Dutch. The English urinate in their own wells, so to speak. They destroy what they came to enjoy. They make matters worse by employing English tradesmen. They pay other English residents to look after their houses. *Mon Dieu*, they bring English food with them. I've seen a kind of viscous brown paste, very salty, they're addicted to, and – O summit of insolence! – they've given it a French name, *la marmite*. They don't even try to speak French, and as for joining in local activities . . . Some don't survive. They sell up and go back home, but they know they won't get their money back if they sell to French buyers, so the property stays in English hands. It's all gone too far. There'll be trouble one day. The Latin fuse isn't very long.

I'm horrified by all this. I can see all kinds of flaws in Eric's arguments, I can see wider economic forces in France at the heart of the same rural depopulation, British or no British, but clearly he feels very deeply about it. I don't try to argue. The Languedoc was always a poor province. Whatever capital trickles into it has always come from outside. Standing beneath the Prieuré cockleshell I apologize for my fellow-countrymen, hoping to placate Eric rather than further antagonise him. Oh, you're all right, he says, more than kindly classing me in a stratum of foreigners who he thinks make positive contributions to the life of the area, if not to his village.

He glances at his watch, exclaims, excuses himself for sounding off and hurries inside to finish off setting up his recording equipment. The Goldberg Ensemble from Vienna is already in there, rehearsing. They're regular visitors, they've been coming to the Prieuré every summer for years. Just now they're rehearsing some French music, a string quartet by Debussy. Ironic, in the circumstances. Another clear case of appropriation.

Will we live here for ever? Who knows? Maybe there's the answer all around us. As far as I know the Languedoc is the only area in the world to be named after a language. Usually it's the other way round. In the days when the original Prieuré was being built and for several centuries afterwards, France was divided linguistically into two. The northern language, the tongue of Paris and its dialects, was known as *langue d'oïl*, after the way they said 'yes'. *Oïl* has since changed into the familiar *oui*. But in the south they said 'oc' for 'yes', something that's been preserved in the name Occitan. So Languedoc is really *langue d'oc*, the tongue or language of 'oc'. Maybe our answer's here: Languedoc – the land that says 'yes'.

I don't think it's any good asking the little man with his hand over his mouth. I expect he knows the answers to all these questions, and many more, but one thing's certain: he's not telling.

Cover Design: Louise Hill
                www.industrialandmarine.com

Layout: Stephen M. L.Young
                latouveilhe@mac.com

Font: Adobe Garamond (11pt)

Printed by: Digisource (GB) Ltd
                1 Chalmers Square
                SW Deans Industrial Estate
                Livingston
                EH54 8RJ
                Scotland
                UK
                www.digisource.co.uk

Published by: Romarin Ltd
                Flat 1
                66 Hencroft St South
                SLOUGH
                SL1 1RE
                United Kingdom

Many thanks to Cynthia St Clair and Philip Humphries, of Bellingham,
Wa., USA, for lending us the photograph from which the drawing on page
62 is adapted.